S0-BYZ-990

Philly Firsts

The Famous, Infamous, and Quirky
of the City of Brotherly Love

Janice L. Booker

YEADON PUBLIC LIBRARY
809 LONGACRE BLVD.
YEADON, PA 19050
(610) 623-4090

Camino Books, Inc.
Philadelphia

974.8
Boo

Copyright © 1999 by Janice L. Booker

All Rights Reserved

No part of this book may be reproduced in any form or by any electronic or mechanical means, including information storage and retrieval systems, without permission in writing from the publisher, except by a reviewer who may quote brief passages in a review.

Manufactured in the United States of America

3 4 5   06 05 04 03

Library of Congress Cataloging-in-Publication Data

Booker, Janice L.
    Philly firsts : the famous, infamous, and quirky of the City of Brotherly
Love / Janice L. Booker.
        p.   cm.
    Includes bibliographical references.
    ISBN 0-940159-44-9   (alk. paper)
    1. Philadelphia (Pa.)—History—Miscellanea.   I. Title.
F158.36.B66   1999
974.8'11—dc21   98-56026

Many of the designations used by manufacturers and sellers to distinguish their products are claimed as trademarks. Where those designations appear in this book, and Camino Books, Inc., was aware of a trademark claim, the designations have been printed in caps or initial caps.

Cover and interior design: Jerilyn Bockorick

This book is available at a special discount on bulk purchases for promotional, business, and educational use.

For information write:
Camino Books, Inc.
P.O. Box 59026
Philadelphia, PA 19102

www.caminobooks.com

To
Ellis, Sam, and George
and
Susan and Jerry

CONTENTS

ACKNOWLEDGMENTS

Writing is a lonely occupation but, for nonfiction writers, also a collaborative one. Bouncing ideas and frustrations around with other writers is always enlightening, and for that help I thank Maxine Abrams, Diana Cavallo, and Ellen Stern. The support and encouragement of friends is energizing. For that support and friendship I thank Gloria Goldberg, Miriam Grimes, Judith Hyman, Lynn Wagman, and Jim Warren. And for a lifetime of understanding and encouragement, for his willingness to withstand temperament and unavailability, I thank, as always, my husband, Al.

For her enthusiasm in researching elusive information, I thank Natalie Shapiro. Kate Treacy's efficiency helped locate the right people in the right places.

Editors walk a tightrope between being a booster and a critic. For her professionalism and dedication to this project, I thank my editor, Carol Hupping. Her questions and comments stretched my own perception of the parameters of this book.

A book that requires this kind of research is dependent on sources. My list of reference books, computer printouts, and interviews necessitated a new file drawer. For help in finding appropriate reference materials, I thank the librarians of the Elkins Park Library and the Jenkintown Library.

Finally, I salute those brave and persistent men and women who helped create this extraordinary city. Philadelphia's firsts have been a vanguard for the nation; its history a microcosm of the grit and enthusiasm that built our wonderful country.

Janice L. Booker

Shame on W. C. Fields and his poor regard for this great city. First prize, he once boldly announced, would be a weekend in Philadelphia, and second prize—a whole week. But even a week would not be enough time to see all the many firsts of which Philadelphia can rightly boast.

The famous artist Gilbert Stuart called Philadelphia "the Athens of America" with good reason. Many of our country's first institutions, now centuries old, still exist here: the first public library, the first university, the first art museum, the first hospital, the first zoo, the first art school, the first public school. . . the list goes on. And let us not forget the many culinary icons that got their start here: Horn & Hardart automats, Tastykakes, Girl Scout cookies, and ice cream.

William Penn imagined his City of Brotherly Love as a "greene countrie towne," and while much of the green has been replaced by concrete and glass, those trees that grace the downtown area are still tall and strong—reminiscent of Penn's vision for a city of homes and thriving commerce. And while William Penn founded the city, it was Benjamin Franklin, more than anyone else, who made it work. Franklin's originality and genius continue to influence science and academic life today. He left us with the Franklin stove, bifocals, the glass armonica, the lightning rod, and the volunteer fire company—all firsts in their day.

From our first Congress to the first computer, politics and technology have been at the forefront of Philadelphia's many contributions to the progress of this nation. So, too, have the city's medical firsts: the hospital, the medical school, the mental institution, and the many medical breakthroughs that have saved lives and brought Philadelphia Nobel Prizes.

The city hasn't lagged behind in celebratory firsts, either. The first World's Fair, which was part of the city's centennial celebration, introduced the telephone and other inventions that paved the way for current technology. The first Thanksgiving Day parade down Philadelphia streets heralded similar events throughout the country. Florists, restaurants, gift shops—and mothers!—are forever grateful to Philadelphia for Mother's Day.

And Philadelphia was not alone. Its creativity and foresight spread throughout the state, as this book's companion volume, *Pennsylvania Firsts* by Patrick M. Reynolds, makes so very clear.

From William Penn's vision of a vital and thriving community to the energetic pursuit of scientific inquiry, Philadelphia is truly a city of firsts. In these pages we salute them.

Politics, Reform, and More Politics

HAPPY BIRTHDAY

The labor pains were intense, but the birth itself was pretty uneventful. When the Declaration of Independence was signed and formally adopted on July 4, 1776, no public announcement was made. The first public reading of the Declaration took place on July 8 at the University of Pennsylvania, then located in the Independence Square area, and was given by university trustee John Nixon (no relation to Richard!). There was a crowd of 8,000, and the Declaration was greeted with hearty and noisy approval. The Liberty Bell rang out to proclaim independence, other bells clanged in unison, and militia guns were sounded to mark the event.

THE FIRST CAPITAL

When the federal government was headquartered in New York in the late 1780s, Philadelphia officials lobbied, offering inducements and bargains, to bring the capital here. The movers and shakers behind the Revolution and Declaration of Independence felt the capital belonged in the (then) most centrally located and wealthiest city in the Union. Opponents grumbled that the contest was to decide which city's taverns would get the most congressional business. The city council made promises: new public buildings and funds for housing for federal officials. (Polishing up the city to attract tourists and business is nothing new!) And it worked, for a while, anyway. In 1790, Philadelphia was declared the first capital of the United States.

The city wanted desperately to become the permanent site of the new nation's capital, and when the federal government agreed to a 10-year "contract" to house the capital in Philadelphia, lawmakers arrived to find a spiffy, cleaned-up city, newly constructed and remodeled buildings, paved streets, and a serious attempt to deodorize the Dock Creek area. But despite all these efforts, the city got only temporary capital status.

A substantial group of influential citizens wanted Germantown to become the capital, but they lost. However, Germantown did serve as the capital for a very brief moment in history. In the autumn of 1793 and the summer of 1794, a yellow fever epidemic turned Philadelphia into a ghost town, with numerous deaths occurring daily. Local doctors who didn't know how to treat the disease responded with bleeding and purging, which of course did no good at all and probably did some harm, since they weakened those already weak with fever. Other physicians, mostly those who had come from the Caribbean and were familiar with the disease, had more of the right idea: they favored fresh air, cleanliness, rest, and a mild diet. People who could flee the city did.

President Washington and most government officials moved to Germantown, and the business of the capital was conducted from the Deshler-Franks-Morris house on Germantown Pike. A committee of prominent local citizens, including merchant Stephen Girard and publisher Mathew Carey, stayed in the city to oversee local affairs.

☞ *To Visit: Deshler Morris House*

Deshler Morris House
5442 Germantown Avenue
Philadelphia, PA 19144
215-596-1748
Hours: April-December: Tuesday-Saturday, 1-4 P.M.
Closed holidays.
Special tours available.
Admission charged.

THE FIRST WHITE HOUSE

The first White House was established at 526-530 High Street (now Market Street). It was owned by Robert Morris, who moved next door to make room for the president and his family. The house already had a history: it had belonged to the wife of Richard Penn, William Penn's grandson. Although President Washington called it "the best single house in the City," he had reservations about its suitability as a presidential mansion, and participated actively in the design of alterations and additions to make it acceptable, using money provided by the city council.

THE ORIGINAL U.S. FLAG

There had been previous American flags, of course, hoisted by the individual colonies, the militia, and various associations. But the new country needed a new flag that united all the former colonies, and no one knew this better than President Washington. There's some controversy about the historical truth of the Betsy Ross story, but many believe it, and believe that something like the following took place:

> George to Martha: Our new country needs a flag. Do you know anybody who could make one?
> Martha to George: Dearest Mr. President, I could suggest my seamstress, Betsy Ross. She lives on Arch Street near Second and she's very creative. But if you use her, make certain she finishes my inaugural gown before she starts on your flag.

A Song for All Reasons

George took Martha's advice and visited Ms. Ross. A passing troubadour eavesdropped on the conversation, and the following is the result:

(To the tune of "Columbia the Gem of the Ocean")

Betsy Ross lived on Arch street near Second
Her sewing was very, very fine.
General Washington paid her a visit
And ordered a brand new flag.
Seven white stripes and six pretty red ones
Thirteen stars on a field of blue,
'Twas the first flag our country ever honored
Three cheers for the red, white and blue.
—Anonymous

☞ *To Visit: Independence National Historical Park*

All our first national shrines—including Independence Hall and the
Betsy Ross House—are located in the area of Independence National
Historical Park.

Independence National Historical Park

313 Walnut Street
Philadelphia, PA 19106
215-597-8974
Independence Hall is open daily, 9 A.M.-5 P.M.
Admission free.

Betsy Ross House

239 Arch Street
Philadelphia, PA 19106
215-627-5343
Hours: Tuesday-Sunday, 10 A.M.-5 P.M.
Admission free.

The first important anti-slavery protest took place on February 18, 1688, by German Quakers. At a meeting in Germantown the Quakers protested "traffic in the bodies of men," and worried about the "lawfulness and

CELEBRATING PATRIOTISM

Following World War II and during the Cold War, the American Heritage Foundation sponsored a project that was sure to stir up patriotism among American citizens. The Freedom Train was inaugurated in Philadelphia on September 17, 1947, and carried 128 historic documents, including the Constitution, the Declaration of Independence, and the Gettysburg Address, among its artifacts. The shiny, seven-car train started its cross-country trip at Broad Street Station, with ceremonies officially dedicating the "caravan of Americanism" on the 160th anniversary of the signing of the U.S. Constitution.

Ceremonies drew 5,000 spectators the first day, with about 35,000 visitors in all. Speeches by government officials and attendance by various organizations enhanced the event. Attendees included 14 European delegates from the International Transport Workers Federation, who were part of a cross-country tour to study American working conditions. Locally, 50 students from the Pennsylvania School for the Deaf and 20 partially sighted students from the Overbrook School for the Blind attended the event. The major address was delivered by U.S. Senator Edward Martin from Pennsylvania. The train stayed in Philadelphia three days before beginning its 30,000-mile tour. It stopped at many cities and towns along the way, each stop accompanied by speeches, media coverage, and spectators.

unlawfulness" of blacks as property. They continued to be concerned with this issue, and in 1696 advised that Friends not encourage the use of blacks as slaves.

Quakers continued to be true to their egalitarian principles when they founded the first antislavery organization in the nation in 1775 in Philadelphia—the Pennsylvania Society for Promoting the Abolition of Slavery, and the Relief of Free Negroes—and made Benjamin Franklin its president. It aided blacks who were freed by their owners and kept records so that proof of their freedom was available to them whenever they needed it.

Abolitionists continued to be active in Philadelphia long after the work of Franklin and the Pennsylvania Society ended. Lucretia Mott was one of these tireless advocates for human rights. In 1868, she organized the Pennsylvania Peace Society, which advanced ideas of binding arbitration, justice to Native Americans, the elimination of military training in schools, and an end to the death penalty—concepts still at the forefront of political and social issues today. A very contemporary-thinking lady!

MINORITIES GET IN THE ACT

The ascension of women and African Americans in the political hierarchy of this country has long been part of Philadelphia's history. In 1938, Crystal Bird Fauset became the first black woman elected to a state legislature. She served in the Pennsylvania House of Representatives for two years. Robert N. C. Nix, Jr., was named chief justice of the Supreme Court of the Commonwealth of Pennsylvania in 1984—the first African American in the country to hold such an office. He retired in 1996. Congressman William J. Gray III was elected to the U.S. House of Representatives in 1979 and became the first African American elected chairman of the influential Budget Committee. He served in that post during the 99th and 100th Congresses. He left Congress in 1991, and

President Harry S. Truman, followed by his cabinet and the members of the Supreme Court, walks next to the Freedom Train, which left Philadelphia to tour the nation in September 1947. *Courtesy of the Free Library of Philadelphia*

President Clinton appointed him special advisor on Haitian affairs in 1994. And Judge Juanita Kidd Stout, who sat on Philadelphia's Municipal Court and Common Pleas Court and the Pennsylvania Supreme Court, was the first African American woman in the nation to be elected a judge.

The first women to become federal government employees were hired way back in 1795 by the U.S. Mint in Philadelphia. Sarah Waldrake and Rachael Summers were hired to weigh gold coins.

PRESIDENTIAL FIRSTS

The first Republican Party national convention took place on June 17, 1856, at Musical Fund Hall in Philadelphia. Here, the first Republican national platform was adopted, and the party nominated presidential candidate John Charles Fremont.

> ### NOT ONE, BUT THREE
>
> It was just as hot inside as outside when, for the first time, three political parties held their national conventions in the same city during the summer of 1948. Philadelphia's Convention Hall, now the Civic Center, hosted the Republican, Democratic, and Progressive Party conventions.

Landmark Debate

Debates have always been an important part of presidential history, but they became more significant when broadcasting entered the picture. The Kennedy-Nixon debates in 1960, the first to be televised, were considered pivotal in swinging the deciding votes to JFK. But the first televised presidential debate between an incumbent and a candidate took place prior to the 1976 election, when the networks worked together to telecast President Gerald Ford and Georgia governor Jimmy Carter at the Walnut Street Theatre. Carter unseated Ford later that year.

MORE FIRSTS

☆ The **Working Men's Party** was organized in July 1828 to represent the working class. (Of course, it was working *men's*, as women didn't get the right to vote until 1920.)

☆ The **first black delegate to a national political convention** was Frederick Douglass. He was present at the National Loyalists' Loyal Union Convention in this city on September 6, 1866.

☆ The **first Women's Declaration of Rights** was presented by Susan B. Anthony in Philadelphia in 1876, during the centennial celebration. Two organizations, the National Woman Suffrage Association and the American Woman Suffrage Association, marched together to disrupt the proceedings (from which they had been denied an official place) and present the declaration.

Let's Celebrate!

FIRST USA BIRTHDAY PARTY

The first birthday of our country was, of course, celebrated in Philadelphia, for the city was the capital of the former colonies. The party was held on July 4, 1777, with ships lined up in the Delaware River discharging 13 cannon shots to honor the 13 brand-new states. But the celebration in 1788 in the birthplace of our Constitution took on mammoth proportions.

The ships *Federal Constitution* and *Union* were mounted on huge wagons drawn by horses with the names of the new states marked on their foreheads. The wagons were driven around the parade area as bells rang out at dawn from Christ Church steeple. The ship *Rising Sun*, at anchor off Market Street, discharged her cannon in salute. All vessels were decorated, and ships were arranged with flags bearing the names of the states.

A grand procession of high-stepping horses pulling a float in the shape of an eagle, its breast emblazoned with 13 stars above 13 red and white stripes, marched proudly around the area we now call Independence National Historical Park. The Constitution was placed upon a staff and crowned with the cap of liberty. Hundreds of citizens marched with their craft or trade society, along with clergy of all faiths. It was reported that 17,000 people participated in the birthday celebrations—a mighty number, considering the city only had a population of about 54,000 at the time. At the end of that day, Benjamin Rush wrote, "'Tis done. We have become a nation."

THANKS FOR THE FIRST THANKSGIVING PARADE

We tip our hats to Gimbel Brothers Department Store, which sponsored the very first Thanksgiving Day parade in Philadelphia in 1920. Even Santa was there; he climbed up the outside of the building to the toy department! Although Gimbels is gone now, Philadelphia's Thanksgiving Day Parade marches on, with varying sponsors, and television coverage. Santa's still part of the parade, but he's not climbing any ladders these days!

COPYCATS

Gimbels' New York City store had opened one block from Macy's on Herald Square in 1910, and it was then that the major rivalry between the two big stores began. Macy's, not to be outdone by its competitor, started its own Thanksgiving Day parade in 1924. Macy's parade has no rivals today; it's the biggest one in the nation. Two and a half million people attended the 1997 parade.

A NATION'S FIRST WORLD'S FAIR

Talk about birthday parties! To mark this country's 100th, Philadelphia hosted the Centennial Exhibition of 1876, the most glamorous and extensive event held anywhere in the world up to that time.

Concrete and Crowds

It was a mammoth show, engineered by John Welsh and a crew of dedicated volunteers. Americans bought shares of stock to help finance the extravaganza. Twenty acres of Fairmount Park's 8,700 acres were covered

Philadelphians and visitors from other states gathered in Fairmount Park in 1876 to celebrate the nation's centennial and inaugurate the first World's Fair. *Courtesy of the Free Library of Philadelphia*

with structures built expressly for the exposition, including Machinery Hall, Memorial Hall, Agricultural Hall, Industrial Hall, the Women's Pavilion, Judges Hall, the Carriage Building, and the Pennsylvania State Building, to name just some. At Horticultural Hall, 80,000 plants were propagated (the beginnings of flower shows to come!). Memorial Hall is the only significant remaining building, its glass and iron dome visible from all parts of the Schuylkill Expressway. The worse the traffic tie-up, the better the view! Of all the state buildings, only Ohio House remains, now used by park rangers. Horticultural Hall still has the original back steps and two outdoor bathrooms, but the hall itself has been rebuilt and now houses the Horticultural Center.

In the exposition's seven months (May through November 1876) it had almost 10 million visitors, who saw displayed the newest and most exciting products and inventions from countries around the world. The Corliss Engine, a 700-ton steam engine installed in the center of Machinery Hall, powered all the mechanically driven exhibits in the building. And the earliest monorail, called "prismoidal," criss-crossed nearby Belmont Avenue, making it one of the Centennial's wonders.

SOCIALIZING IN A CLUBBY TOWN

Exclusive clubs have long been a standard in Philadelphia society; among the earliest were the fishing clubs located along several miles of the Schuylkill River. The State in Schuylkill Fishing Company, also known as the State in Schuylkill, was founded in 1732 by prominent area citizens and was then called the Colony of Schuylkill. After the American Revolution, the word *colony* was changed to *state*.

A SPECIAL PUNCH INVENTED

Fish House Punch was invented in 1732 at the State in Schuylkill Fishing Company. Tradition has it that this special punch starts every meeting, and that one of the imbibers of this drink was President Washington.

As industrialization grew, the river became home to the city gas works, oil refineries, slaughterhouses that dumped refuse into the water, and several manufacturing firms. The river became polluted from unrestricted dumping, forcing the club to move to the banks of the Delaware. Eventually it became a dining club. The clubhouse, called "the castle," was physically moved several times to various locations, until it settled at its present site in Andalusia, next to the Biddle Estate. The State in Schuylkill still exists, still an exclusive dining club, its members keeping it private and select. Strictly for men, the group occasionally schedules gourmet dinners. New members are the waiters; considering the exclusivity of the club, we can be certain that CEOs of major companies are scuttling about with trays. Maintaining old rituals, toasts are offered to President Washington and Governor Morris.

Another such club, Fort St. David's Fishing Company, may have been Pennsylvania's first museum; it housed a very early collection of Indian materials and objects of natural history. Fort St. David's was absorbed by the State in Schuylkill. For those wealthy men who chose a sport other than fishing, the Jockey Club was founded here in 1766 "to encourage the breeding of good horses and to promote the pleasures of the turf."

DANCING IN THE DARK

The year was 1893, and "Professor" Harry and Annie Wagner founded the first ballroom and dancing academy in America at 44 North Fourth Street. Eventually, Wagner's Ballroom became a fixture in the Olney section of the city. It was a popular meeting place for Saturday night dances—a precursor to today's singles spots.

The Wagners' grandson, Joseph H. Smith, managed the dance hall for many years, and it became *the* place to dance in Philadelphia. The traditional fox trot gave way to the Twist, and during the 1960s, when disc jockey Jerry Blavat emceed the dances, as many as 1,500 youngsters from across the city came to dance. After being in business for 77 years, Wagner's Ballroom closed its doors for good in 1970.

COLONISTS PARTY

The first recorded formal social event was organized by the Assembly Dancing Society in 1749, probably in preparation for Philadelphia's debutante balls. The familiar austere and somber clothing of the Quakers was not yet in vogue, and women appeared in public in bright colors. Although not dancers themselves, the Quakers were not opposed to the dancing assemblies, which attracted the wealthier merchants and landowners of colonial Philadelphia. Dancing masters were hired to teach "fashionable English and French dances." Some people attended who did not dance; they spent the evening playing cards. In fact, invitations to these events were printed on the undecorated sides of playing cards.

Eventually these balls became subscription events. Forty shillings admitted a gentleman and his date to 16 or 18 dancing evenings. The price of admission included punch (heavy with rum and 200 limes) and a bread basket. The evenings began at 6 P.M. and ended by midnight. Dances were presented every Thursday night in winter and early spring.

SOCIAL STRATA OBSERVED

The dancing assemblies were highly aristocratic; wives and daughters of common laborers were not allowed into this social scene. A seating order, dictated by the directors, was rigidly observed.

A NEW KIND OF EXTRAVAGANZA

Back in 1792, John Bill Ricketts constructed a building at 12th and Market Streets to house the first riding academy. Ricketts was an ambitious man, and he started a circus the following year. Ricketts' Circus wasn't too different from what we see today: tumblers, acrobats, fancy horsemanship. The show was a rousing success, attracting between 600 and 700 patrons to every performance. Even President Washington attended! Soon Ricketts had to move to larger quarters at Sixth and Chestnut Streets. Although his circus was the first of its kind in the nation and attracted big audiences, Ricketts didn't give up the riding academy; horsemanship lessons continued in the morning and the circus performances took place in the evening.

Forever the entrepreneur, Ricketts soon opened a coffee shop on the premises. In 1795, he built an amphitheater in New York City to house his circus, and two years later he took his show on the road, exhibiting in towns as far north as Albany. The Sixth and Chestnut Street building in Philadelphia was destroyed by fire in 1799 and was never rebuilt.

THE BEGINNINGS OF MOTHER'S DAY

At a public meeting in 1907, Anna Jarvis of Philadelphia proposed that on the second Sunday in May everyone wear a carnation to commemorate mothers. She suggested wearing a pink or red carnation if your mother was living, and a white one if your mother was deceased.

The idea of honoring mothers on a day dedicated to peace was originally proposed in 1872 by Julia Ward Howe (who wrote the words to "The Battle Hymn of the Republic"). Jarvis started a campaign to make it happen, spearheading a letter-writing drive to ministers, businessmen, and politicians.

MOTHERS WANT FLOWERS

According to the Society of American Florists, Mother's Day ranks second only to Christmas as the biggest day of the year to send gifts of plants and flowers. And that's what mothers want more than anything else on their day: 40 percent prefer flowers, outranking all other gift options, says the International Council of Shopping Centers.

Jarvis was never a mother herself, but her campaign was successful, and it began a nationwide observance. Philadelphia was the first city to adopt the Mother's Day proposal in 1908, and in 1914, President Woodrow

Wilson proclaimed the day a national holiday. Mother's Day is enthusiastically celebrated in this country, as you well know if you've ever tried to get a last-minute dinner reservation on that day! According to restaurateurs, it's the most popular day of the year for dining out. The observance of Mother's Day has spread throughout the world—to England, France, Sweden, Denmark, India, China, and Mexico, where the celebration lasts not one but two days.

MUM'S NOT THE WORD FOR THE MUMMERS

Not only the first but still unique among New Year's celebrations, the Philadelphia Mummers Parade has been exciting spectators since the late 1700s. We can thank the Swedes for its beginnings, for they brought with them to the New World their custom of visiting friends on "Second Day Christmas," December 26. The celebration was extended to the New Year, with masquerades and parades. The sounds of pistols and muskets soon joined the bells and noisemakers to welcome in the new year, naming the revelers the New Year's Shooters and Mummers Association.

Mummers, in all their finery, gather to prepare for yet another New Year's Day Parade.
Courtesy of the Mummers Museum

Traveling Troubadours

Groups traveled from house to house performing songs and dances and were rewarded with food and drink. By 1808 the revelry was so widespread, Philadelphia high society considered the noise and noisemakers a problem. Authorities imposed a law declaring "masquerades, masquerade balls, and masked processions to be public nuisances!" Threats of fine and imprisonment quieted the celebrations but did not stop them, and in the 1850s, the law was repealed.

By 1870, with the nation recuperating from the Civil War, the loosely organized neighborhood celebrations evolved into a parade featuring fancy dress clubs and comic clubs. By 1901, the parade was officially sponsored by the city. The next year, string bands joined the group, and in the 1970s the Fancy Brigades took on their own identity, separate from the Fancy Clubs. Four divisions exist today: the Comics, the Fancies, the String Bands, and the Fancy Brigades.

The Comics start the parade. Their themes are satire and humor. They also wear the oldest costumes of the Mummers, often modified colonial dress. Clowns are an important part of the Comics. The Fancies are composed of individual performances, small groups such as trios, or some juveniles. Their costumes are large and elaborate, some built over wooden frames and extending as high as 15 feet. The 19 clubs of the String Band division are the only Mummers who play instruments as part of their presentations, using their own themes. The Fancy Brigades are composed of 14 clubs, each of which has between 35 and 100 members. Each club's performance revolves around a central theme.

For many years, participants had such a good time, they kept the celebration going until after New Year's. But in 1901, when the Mummers were organizing themselves into clubs and the city was lighting City Hall for the first time, the city administration invited the Mummers to march more formally on New Year's Day, with an offering of $25 to each club. After that, the parade was confined to January 1.

A Year to Prepare

Before New Year's Day ends, preparations for the following year begin, including formulating theme ideas and designing costumes. For many years, the intricate sewing and beading was done by the Mummers' families. The task has taken on enormous proportions. Some costumes are still painstakingly created by families and other volunteers, and ongoing fund-raising activities pay for the very costly costumes. Beads, feathers, satin capes, and floats are expensive; some individual costumes cost as much as $5,000!

NOT JUST WHITE MALES ANYMORE

For much of their history, the Mummers were all male. As the city expanded, both in population and ethnic composition, the Mummers' ranks expanded to include women, African Americans, and a cross-section of the many ethnic groups that live in the city. Even geographically, things have changed. At first, the clubs were based primarily in South Philadelphia; now, the Mummers come from all over the city and the tri-state area.

The parade used to be mere entertainment—spectacularly costumed participants doing the famous "Mummers Strut" to the tune of "Oh, Dem Golden Slippers." Now there's also social commentary, with burlesques and parodies of current issues and public figures. The Comics poke fun at everyone and everything. Mummers gather before dawn to get ready to march until after dark down Broad Street. They're joined by thousands of spectators, many of whom also get up in the darkness of early morning on New Year's Day so they can beat the crowds and get a front-row spot along Broad Street.

Twenty thousand Mummers march three miles along the parade route. Judges view the parade from prime seats and award prizes to participating clubs. An innovation was recently introduced: the Fancy Brigades paraded in the Convention Center for the judges after they completed their Broad Street stint. Spectators were willing to pay an admission charge so they could sit indoors, out of the cold New Year's Day weather. The city's Department of Recreation co-sponsors the parade and awards monetary prizes for the best in each category.

☞ To Visit: Philadelphia Mummers Museum

Because the Mummers are a famous Philadelphia tradition, the Mummers Museum was built to display their history, sights, and sounds. Featured are old costumes, sounds of string bands, and videos of past parades. The museum also houses a research library of documents and a large collection of costume design sketches.

Philadelphia Mummers Museum
Second Street at Washington Avenue
Philadelphia, PA 19147
215-336-3050
Hours: Tuesday-Saturday, 9:30 A.M.-5 P.M.; Sunday, 12-5 P.M.
Closed Sundays in July and August.
Admission charged.

IT'S A BLOOMIN' WORLD

What would March be in Philadelphia without the flower show? Thousands cram into the new convention center to flee the last of winter, even if only for a few hours, and to view the extravagant blooms, bushes, and botanical wonders awaiting them inside.

THE NUMBERS INCREASE

The Philadelphia Flower Show runs for eight days and attracts more than 200,000 people.

The exhibitions, sponsored by the Pennsylvania Horticultural Society, were first seen by the public in Philadelphia in June 1829 in Masonic Hall on Chestnut Street. The Horticultural Society, which organized in November 1827 in the Hall of the Franklin Institute, first exhibited its own unusual flowers, plants, and fruits to members, then relocated to the Society Hill area.

The First Flowers

The Pennsylvania Horticultural Society is the oldest continually operating horticultural society in the United States. Indeed, as far as anyone can discern, the Philadelphia show was the first flower show of any size or consequence held in the country. Celebrated annually in May or June until 1832, it then was moved to September and now takes place in early March, as the harbinger of spring.

The site of the flower show has moved as Philadelphia has grown. Once held in the old Commercial Museum, then at the Civic Center (the refurbished Convention Hall), it now takes place at the Pennsylvania Convention Center.

EARLY BLOOMERS

The first Philadelphia Flower Show as we now know it blossomed in 1966 in the new, partially completed Civic Center. The larger space was a great improvement, but evidently someone didn't like the harsh ceilings: the following year, 6,000 yards of gold and beige satin were draped over them to soften the atmosphere.

Producing the Philadelphia Flower Show takes more than imagination and talent; it also takes special gardening know-how. Preparation for each show begins three years in advance. And 50 tractor-trailerloads of mulch are brought in so that the more than one million plants forced into early flowering can be set above the concrete floor.

☞ To Visit: Philadelphia Flower Show

Pennsylvania Horticultural Society
100 North 20th Street
Philadelphia, PA 19103
215-988-8800

MORE FIRSTS

☆ The **first balloon flight** in the nation was a 40-minute excursion from Philadelphia to Deptford Township, New Jersey, a distance of about 15 miles. It took place on January 9, 1793. President Washington watched the ascent and placed a presidential order on the hot air balloon, giving permission for the flight. Piloted by a Frenchman, Jean-Pierre Blanchard, the balloon soared about one mile into the sky.

☆ The **first merry-go-round** was produced in 1867 by a German-born Philadelphian, Gustav A. Dentzel, whose family had made carousels in Germany. He opened a shop as a cabinet maker but wanted to test the American public's reaction to his merry-go-round. The response was enthusiastic, and he became the most famous steam-and-horsepower-carousel carver and manufacturer in the United States. Dentzel took his carousel from town to town, and by 1880, competition had begun in the field of merry-go-round manufacturing.

☆ Our country's **sesqui-centennial** (150th anniversary) celebration in 1926 was quite an affair, thanks in great part to business magnate John Wanamaker, who proposed the event. There was an international exposition, concerts, aerial demonstrations, fireworks, and an inaugural ball. The Liberty Bell was illuminated and could be seen all the way down Broad Street. Unfortunately, spirits and events were dampened by rain that fell on 107 of the 184 days of the exposition.

☆ The **bicentennial** celebration in 1976 generated many firsts in Philadelphia, including the restoration of many city landmarks: Independence National Historical Park, Franklin Court, the Liberty Bell Pavilion, the Visitors Center, old City Tavern, and the Penn's Landing area. All of these are still used by Philadelphians and visitors.

It's the Law

A NEW KIND OF PRISON

Although construction began in 1822, Eastern State Penitentiary opened in 1829. In continuous use until its closing in 1971, it was the first U.S. prison built with reform and rehabilitation—not merely punishment—as its goals. But you'd never know it by looking at its exterior, with its forbidding, castle-like turrets and towering, massive stone walls. The penal reformers of the day believed that such a formidable facade would send a strong message to would-be criminals on the outside and provide few clues to the interior space, which, based on solitary confinement, provided a civilized environment for those imprisoned there.

Before this time, most punishment of criminals was a public event involving flogging, stocks, or some other corporal method. Prison reformers, particularly Philadelphia Quakers, wanted a more humane way to punish offenders, one that resulted in penance, rehabilitation, and discouragement of future criminal behavior.

Design Means Redemption

British architect John Haviland's design for Eastern State was based on ecclesiastical views of redemption achieved through isolation. The prison was to operate somewhat like a monastery, except that the inhabitants were unwilling participants!

Corridors containing individual cells radiated from a central core. Openings in the corridor walls allowed food and work materials to be

Built as a model prison based on solitary confinement, Eastern State Penitentiary was considered revolutionary in concept, but it just didn't work. *Courtesy of Eastern State Penitentiary Museum*

passed through, and there were peepholes so guards could observe prisoners. Each cell contained a bed, a tap for fresh water, vents for heating and fresh air, and a primitive toilet. A small skylight in the vaulted ceiling permitted outside light to come through.

FOR THE PENITENT

The root of the word *penitentiary* is *penitent,* and it means providing an opportunity for an offender to be penitent, or sorry for his wrongdoing, and consequently reform.

The castle-like stone facade of Eastern State Penitentiary was designed to discourage criminal activities that would mean imprisonment behind its walls. *Courtesy of Eastern State Penitentiary Museum*

After the prison opened, officials discovered that the original plan of 250 cells was inadequate, so four two-story cell blocks were built. Adjustments were made throughout the years of construction and when the prison was finally completed in 1836, it housed about 450 prisoners, all in solitary confinement. At that time, Eastern State was the largest public structure in the country.

The daily regimen, with its focus on no communication between prisoners and guards, consisted of a daybreak awakening, three meals, and bed by 9 or 10 P.M. Exercise in the individual yards was permitted one hour a day, with staggered hours to prevent any opportunity for conversation with a neighbor. Prisoners were addressed by number, not name, to foster anonymity.

Criticism and Commentary

The prison's elaborate construction and design brought fame to the architect and both accolades and criticism to the state. Many critics maintained that health problems would be exacerbated by the primitive conditions and that solitary confinement would promote mental illness. Charles Dickens, after a visit, described the system of solitary confinement as "cruel and wrong," and thought it inhumane.

Yet Cherry Hill, as the prison was nicknamed because of the cherry orchard on the site, became the prototype for many prisons worldwide, both in design and in philosophy. The design was duplicated by more than 300 prisons throughout the world, and Eastern State Penitentiary was considered the first step to a new and progressive penal reform.

Although innovative and original, the new ideas of rehabilitation didn't work. Penal authorities still struggle, as they did in the days of Eastern State, to find rehabilitation methods that reduce parolees' return to crime and reduce crime in general. Investigations of conditions and treatment of prisoners at Eastern State continued, and the experiment was ultimately regarded as a failure. After 142 years of operation, Eastern State Penitentiary is now a museum.

Fame to the Architect

Haviland's design for Eastern State brought him national and international fame; he was hired to design many public buildings in Philadelphia, as well as other penitentiaries throughout the country.

CREATIVE ESCAPES

Despite Eastern State Penitentiary's massive construction, prisoners found ways to escape. The most notorious of these escapades occurred in April 1945, via a tunnel, and involved 22 men. Most escapees were caught the same day—including Willie Sutton, the infamous bank robber.

🖝 *To Visit: Eastern State Penitentiary*

Eastern State Penitentiary
22nd Street and Fairmount Avenue
Philadelphia, PA 19130
215-236-3300
Call for hours open to the public.
Children under 7 not admitted.
Admission charged.

LAWYERS GET EDUCATED

The first university law professorship in the United States was established at the University of Pennsylvania Law School in 1790 by James Wilson. But what good is a school without access to a library? In 1802, the first U.S. law library was inaugurated by the Philadelphia Bar Association.

And what's a library without books? The first law library must surely have had on its shelves the first law book published in America, written by none other than William Penn himself. Its title seems endless: it begins *The Excellent Priviledge* [sic] *of Liberty and Property being the birth-right of the free-born subjects of England...* and continues on for a number of sentences, outlining the contents of the book.

Also on the shelves must have been the first American law dictionary, published in two volumes in 1839. It, too, had a formidable title: *A Law Dictionary Adapted to the Constitution and Laws of the United States of America and of the Several States of the American Union With References to the Civil and Other Systems of Foreign Law.*

LAWYERS GET ORGANIZED

The American Bar Association (ABA) was organized in 1878. Its forerunner was the Philadelphia Bar Association, established in 1802 by fewer than 100 lawyers. Instrumental in the national organization was Francis Rawle, a descendant of the founder of the oldest law firm in the nation, which, naturally, was in Philadelphia.

Lawyers and Meetings

In 1878, a group of lawyers from 29 states joined Philadelphia lawyer Francis Rawle at Saratoga Springs, New York, to make his vision of a national organization of lawyers a reality. No member had considered bringing a gavel to call the meeting to order, so Rawle purchased a carpenter's mallet at a local hardware store for 17 cents.

Today, the original gavel, silver- and gold-plated and embossed with the names of many ABA past presidents, symbolizes the ABA and is on display at the Bar Association Museum at the association's headquarters in Chicago. It was used for about 70 years, but the size and heavy metal plating made it cumbersome, so a replica in sterling silver is now used to call meetings to order.

The carpenter's mallet purchased by Francis Rawle and used as a gavel by the American Bar Association from 1878 to 1946. *Photograph from the book* A Good Day at Saratoga *by Gerald Carson, courtesy of the American Bar Association Museum of Law*

WHO'S ON FIRST?

What's in a date? The Philadelphia Bar Association considers itself the oldest chartered bar association in the country, yet the Boston bar claims it's the oldest. Newspaper accounts of the issue call the Philadelphia Bar Association the oldest chartered metropolitan bar association. The disagreement continues and is argued at law conferences to this day.

To set the record straight, Boston may have the oldest chartered bar association, but Philadelphia's was the first to formally organize. Although meetings were held in Boston in 1763, the group had no charter then. By 1770, participants had agreed to meet regularly in a tavern, but formal organization of the Boston bar came after 1802, the year Philadelphia lawyers had their official start. Back in 1784, a society of Philadelphia law students and young lawyers banded together as the Society for the Promotion of Legal Knowledge and Forensic Excellence; the Philadelphia bar points to that meeting as its unofficial beginning.

THE FIRST LAW FIRM

The Philadelphia Bar Association goes back a long way, and so do law firms, or at least one law firm: Rawle & Henderson is recognized as the oldest law firm in the United States, operating continuously since 1783. It was founded by William Rawle as a one-man practice, and it has continued through generations of Rawles. By the way, Benjamin Franklin figures prominently in the firm's history. In 1721, as an apprentice printer, Franklin printed a treatise written by Francis Rawle. It was Franklin's first book.

A PHILADELPHIA LAWYER

The phrase "a Philadelphia lawyer" has been with us for a long time. Webster defines it as "a lawyer of outstanding ability at exploiting legal fine points and technicalities." How did this phrase originate? In 1734, John Peter Zenger was arrested for sedition, libel, and falsehoods by the governor of

New York, who was infuriated by Zenger's published accusations of election irregularities. An out-of-state lawyer was sought to handle the defense so that there would be no suspicion of political influence. Philadelphia attorney Andrew Hamilton was chosen, and when Zenger was found not guilty, Hamilton became known respectfully as the "Philadelphia lawyer."

MORE FIRSTS

☆ Many historians contend that the **first treaty with local Indian tribes** was made between William Penn and the Shackamaxon Indians in 1682. It was thought that Penn gave a speech at the time the treaty was made, but he actually did not deliver it until 20 years later. Nonetheless, the treaty remains one of Penn's early symbols of authority in the New World. Original documents affirming the existence of this treaty are long lost, but it is a fact that Penn paid the Indians for land through treaties such as this; many other settlers did not. Actually, Penn was one of the few gentlemen who tried to deal fairly with Native Americans.

☆ The **first United States Supreme Court Building** was erected in 1791 in Philadelphia. Originally intended to be a city hall, it was an architectural match for the building where the U.S. Congress first met.

☆ The **first recorded kidnapping for ransom** occurred on July 1, 1874, in Germantown, when four-year-old Charles Brewster Ross was held for $20,000 ransom. Friends of the child's father collected the money, but the police persuaded the family to offer it as a reward for the capture of the kidnappers and the return of the child instead. Two robbers were apprehended and shot in New York later that year and one confessed to the kidnapping, saying that only his companion knew the whereabouts of the child. But his partner was already dead from his gunshot wound, and the boy was never found.

☆ The **first black judge of a circuit court of appeals** was William Henry Hastie. He was confirmed by the U.S. Senate on July 19, 1950, and appointed to the Third Judicial Circuit Court. Hastie, who had been governor of the U.S. Virgin Islands, was sworn in in Philadelphia.

Money Money Money

FIRST FINANCIAL HEART OF THE NATION

The Philadelphia Stock Exchange first opened its doors in 1754, making it the first American stock exchange. Business was conducted informally, to say the least. Almost all transactions took place at City Tavern, already a well-established gathering place for merchants. It wasn't until 1790 that securities brokers left the tavern for new offices and established the Philadelphia Board of Brokers. By then, Philadelphia was the financial heart of the young nation.

Stocks may have been traded in the City of Brotherly Love, but New York was the business center of the nation, and speeding coaches regularly dashed from New York to Philadelphia, carrying speculators and stock-jobbers, foreign investors and inside traders.

First and Fast

Some shrewd Philadelphia brokers, determined to beat their rivals, set up an innovative signaling system that transmitted key information from New York to Philadelphia much faster than any other means at the time. They put up signal stations on high points across New Jersey and hired signalmen to watch them through telescopes. It was each signalman's job to decipher coded flashes of light that carried news of stock prices, lottery numbers, and other financial information and send it on to the next station, where another signalman waited. Relayed from station to station, this news could get from New York to Philadelphia in as

The paperwork generated by today's Philadelphia Stock Exchange must move figures along faster than the signal system originally used to transmit information! *Courtesy of the Philadelphia Stock Exchange*

little as 10 minutes, beating by hours the arrival of the speculators in their coaches! This system was so efficient that it remained in use until the telegraph became widely used in the 1840s.

ALWAYS WITH US

We hate to pay insurance premiums, but we love to know that we're protected financially. Our forefathers must have felt the same way. The first fire insurance company, the Philadelphia Contributionship, was organized in 1752 and chartered as the "Insurance of Houses from Loss by Fire" in 1768. The company had to be confirmed by George III, the king of England, on the advice of his Privy Council at the Court of St. James. The first name subscribed to the deed of settlement, or articles of association, was James Hamilton, Lieutenant Governor of the Province; the first private name was Benjamin Franklin. (Wasn't he the wise old owl to get fire insurance, considering all those experiments with electricity?) The first policy was issued on June 1, 1752, to John Smith of Philadelphia—who, for a whopping one dollar, insured his house, which was valued at $1,000.

First Came the Volunteers

Philadelphia's volunteer fire companies, whose members remained volunteers until 1871, when the city began to pay its firefighters, were the first in the United States. Insurance seemed a natural outgrowth of their activities, and they helped Benjamin Franklin organize the Philadelphia Contributionship. Insurance companies benefitted subscribers by offering rewards to encourage the volunteers. Several brigades raced to be first on the scene when the fire alarm sounded, because the first to put out the fire reaped the reward.

Burning Issues

Just as they do today, insurance companies inspected each building for structural integrity and safety before issuing insurance. After Edward Shippen's house was damaged by fire, all policyholders were required to attach badges to their properties so that everyone (most importantly, the firefighters!) could see that the property was indeed insured.

Shippen was a prominent citizen—president of the Court of Common Pleas of Philadelphia County and eventually chief justice of Pennsylvania (he was also the father-in-law of the notorious Benedict Arnold). Perhaps it was his eminent position that prompted more serious attention to house fires; in any case, we have Shippen to thank for fire insurance. Because he was such an important citizen, his house fire prompted civic-minded individuals to consider the damage fire caused, and probably made them worry more about their own properties. After the Shippen fire, the Philadelphia Contributionship issued the following statement: "The Directors observ[ed] that much of the Damage was done thro' Indiscretion, which they think might have been prevented had it appear'd by the Badge being placed up to Notify that the sd. House was so immediately under their Care...." This seemed to be a not-so-discreet reminder that to those houses that carried the badge, indicating owners were insured, more immediate attention might be paid by the firefighters.

Badges Still Issued

Some homes in Chestnut Hill and Center City, remainders of colonial construction, still sport the badges, but they're only historical curiosities now. The first badges, called the "hand in hand" symbol, showed four clasped, gilded hands. The marks were made of lead and mounted on a wooden shield. As other fire insurance companies came into existence, other fire marks were designed; some show a tree, others an eagle. The fire department didn't look first, before it got out the hoses, although legend has it that the volunteers were not so eager to douse a fire when they saw no plaques, because they couldn't be sure that a reward would be forthcoming. Of course, no firefighter looks for the fire badge today, but the Contributionship continues to issue fire marks to its policyholders, and many are still placed upon homes.

Life Insurance Follows

The first life insurance company, the Presbyterian Ministers Fund, was established in 1717. At that time, insurance was limited to Presbyterian

These clasped hands appear as the fire mark on the plaques issued by the Philadelphia Contributionship when it was the first fire insurance company, and they are still issued today to the insured. *Photograph by Will Brown, courtesy of The Philadelphia Contributionship for the Insurance of Houses from Loss by Fire (The Contributionship)*

ministers and their widows who had fallen on hard times, so it was really more of a charitable organization, and the fund was independently operated by the presbytery. After the Constitution was adopted, the fund was incorporated and organized along the lines of secular insurance companies, with premiums purchased by the insured. By the late Victorian period, the fund was selling insurance to other denominations, and in the early 20th century, to anyone. In the 1960s, the company was sold to a commercial life insurance company.

The first true life insurance company, as we know them today, was the Pennsylvania Company for Insurances on Lives and Granting Annuities. A group of businessmen gathered for lunch at City Tavern in December 1809 to discuss setting up a company to insure lives and grant annuities.

Companies that sold marine and fire insurance had been around for some time, but life insurance was unheard of in the United States.

Jacob Shoemaker, a Philadelphia businessman who pastured his cows in what today is Washington Square, at Sixth and Walnut Streets in the Independence National Historical Park area, was the driving force here. He felt that life insurance would add to the economic security of the growing community. Shoemaker was very conscious of his own economic well-being; the city corporation didn't charge him for the use of his pasture until complaints from the neighbors forced its hand.

But Shoemaker was more than a farmer. As a citizen and a patriot, he was disturbed by American dependence on British companies for life insurance protection. (He was also a life insurance broker.) He and Joseph Ball, another influential businessman, were instrumental in the formation of the first life insurance company in America.

LOCAL BANKS AREN'T ENOUGH

Both Alexander Hamilton and Robert Morris (considered by many to be the financier of the American Revolution) knew that once the American colonies became a nation they would need a national banking system; indeed, it came to be.

In 1780, the Pennsylvania Bank, headquartered in Philadelphia, became the first bank authorized by the Continental Congress. The Pennsylvania Bank became the Bank of North America, the first incorporated bank chartered by the Continental Congress, on December 31, 1781. The first president of the Bank of North America was Robert Morris, who was appointed the nation's superintendent of finance in 1781. (The title of that office was changed to secretary of the Treasury before Hamilton assumed the position.) In 1787, when the Constitutional Convention met in Philadelphia, the Bank of North America, the Massachusetts Bank, and the Bank of New York were the only banks in existence. It was clear that more banks were needed to satisfy the growing needs of the new country.

Banks Go National

The First Bank of the United States was founded to help finance the new federal government. It was chartered in 1791 (subscriptions were first received on July 4 of that year in the Bank of North America on Chestnut Street), and construction of its building began in 1795. Shares were sold and the bank opened branches in other cities, but Congress refused to renew its charter in 1811 because it believed that banking should be left to the individual states.

The First Bank was the only national commercial bank in the country, and the methods it used in central banking started the Federal Reserve System. From its beginnings, this bank served as the fiscal agent of the government through its close association with the Treasury Department. Because of its branches throughout the infant nation, it was a national institution in its operations and influence, and due to its conservative management, the bank acted as a restraint over other banks in the country in maintaining a proper credit balance.

The imposing facade of the First Bank of the United States, constructed between 1795 and 1797 on Third Street, south of Chestnut, now across from the Visitors Center. *Photograph by Ted Rosenberg*

More and More Banks

After this initiation, banks blossomed. The Philadelphia Saving Fund Society (PSFS), established on December 2, 1816, was the first mutual savings bank in the country. Much of the credit for starting this bank goes to Condy Raguet, a native Philadelphian of French descent, who was its driving force. When it began, PSFS was located at 22 South Sixth Street, which was the office of George Billington, who became its first secretary-treasurer.

Banks such as PSFS provided one model for different types of banking institutions that were popping up all over the country. A system of national banks grew out of the federal government's need to establish a market for its bonds (which it began selling to raise money to pay the large debts it had incurred during the Civil War). The first charter was granted to the First National Bank of Philadelphia on June 30, 1863, by the National Banking Act.

Home Financing

But all of these banks, from high finance to savings, were missing one element: they didn't sell mortgages. When a factory worker, postman, or lamplighter wanted to build a house, there was no bank that could help him finance it. Not, at least, until 1831, when he could approach the first building and loan association.

A meeting on January 3 of that year was held for the purpose of "forming an association to enable contributors thereof to build or purchase dwelling houses." The Oxford Provident Building Association of Philadelphia County, on Frankford Avenue in the Northeast (at that time called Frankford, Pennsylvania), became the first building and loan association in the United States. It was just the first of many.

THE FIRST U.S. MINT

David Rittenhouse, a professor and vice-provost at the University of Pennsylvania (and great-grandson of William Rittenhouse), designed and built the machinery and dies for making U.S. coins. He became the first director of the U.S. Mint when it was founded in 1792. In those early days the mint had a horse-powered rolling mill, which was converted to steam power in 1833.

President Washington himself supervised the building of the mint, probably because it was the first government-owned building. In fact, Washington felt so strongly about the mint that he is believed to have contributed some of his personal silver for minting. The Mint Act of April 2, 1792, was essential to the financial structure of the country; it instituted the first standardized U.S. coin, which would replace the many different means of exchange that were in circulation at the time. In the early days of the colonies, barter was used a lot. Later, each state issued its own paper money, called continentals, and coins called shillings and pence were used. When the Articles of Confederation (1778) specifically mandated a standardized system of coinage, a decimal system was established that started at $ .01 and went to $10.00.

FOREIGN EXCHANGE

The U.S. Mint was busy not only with American money but with foreign currency as well. In 1874, Congress authorized the mint to produce coins for foreign countries. The U.S. Mint made coins for Venezuela in 1876, and following the Spanish-American War, it minted coins for Mexico, Panama, Peru, and the Philippines.

In 1801, the U.S. Mint produced silver peace medals that were presented to American Indians to solidify peace treaty negotiations. The coins pictured the face of the current president, Thomas Jefferson. Thus began the tradition of the Presidential Medal series.

DOWN BY THE RIVERSIDE

The patriarch of Philadelphia's influential Rittenhouse family, William Rittenhouse, built the first paper mill in the country in 1690. The site was a rivulet called Paper Mill Run, just a few miles north of the junction of the Schuylkill and Wissahickon Rivers. The paper was made by hand: linen rags were pounded into pulp in stone mortars, then each sheet was made separately. Rittenhouse's paper mill was the first, but not the last, factory to be built along the Wissahickon; eventually, 60 industries were strung along its banks.

FINANCING EDUCATION

The Wharton School of Finance and Commerce was the first business school in the country, established at the University of Pennsylvania in 1881. Joseph Wharton, the iron manufacturer who founded Bethlehem Steel Company, gave the university $100,000 to found his namesake, where today's graduates number among the most visible and influential CEOs and financial experts in the country.

ROLL OUT THE CARPETS

American interior design is indebted to William Peter Sprague, who founded the first carpet mill in this country on North Second Street in 1791. His hand looms were used to manufacture Axminster carpets. Sprague liked to concentrate on patriotic designs, and one of his earliest carpets reproduced the aims and achievements of the republic. Carpet manufacture was modeled after the garment industry: manufacturers took orders for work and set up looms in workers' homes. It became a thriving cottage industry; by 1850, there were about 100 carpet manufacturers in the Philadelphia area.

GETTING ORGANIZED

Before the days of labor unrest and unions, the first trade associations were really price-fixing groups within particular trades, and they attempted to guarantee high-quality products. They were multi-purpose, providing insurance for members and educated apprentices. These associations included both masters and journeymen, because the mechanics believed their interests were the same as their employers': if prices were high, wages would follow. Journeymen also established separate mutual-aid societies, following social lines. The Carpenters' Company of Philadelphia was founded in 1724 as a price-fixing association, probably composed only of master builders.

Sometimes Strikes Clear the Air

The first recorded strike of wage earners occurred in 1786, when Philadelphia printers struck for a minimum wage of six dollars a week. They won. In May 1791, the Journeymen Carpenters of the City and Liberties of Philadelphia struck against master carpenters for a 10-hour working day—the first strike about hours in the nation. They lost.

The shoemakers of Philadelphia composed the first ongoing organization of wage earners. It started in 1792 but lasted less than a year, then reorganized in 1794 as the Federal Society of Journeymen Cordwainers, which existed until 1806 (*cordwainers* meant "cobblers"). This organization was indicted twice on conspiracy charges, but it was the first local union of wage earners organized to maintain or advance wages through collective bargaining.

Unions Grow Stronger

The American labor movement began in this city in 1827, when the Mechanics Union of Trade Associations was organized and all trade societies were invited to join. In June 1827, 600 journeymen carpenters again struck for a 10-hour day, precipitating a general movement for shorter hours. The Mechanics Union went out of existence in 1829, but from its emphasis on nominating sympathetic political candidates emerged the Working Men's Party, organized in 1828.

The first union to admit anyone other than master craftsmen was formed in 1847 by crusading journalist George Lippard. The Brotherhood of the Union established itself as a secret society, full of rituals and robes, and continued into the 20th century. This union set up branches in other states, and is regarded by some historians as the parent organization of the Noble Order of the Knights of Labor, founded in Philadelphia in 1869.

Carpenters' Company Still Exists

Modeled after medieval craft guilds, the Carpenters' Company still owns and maintains the building on Chestnut Street across from Franklin Court that was the site of the Continental Congress in 1774, as well as other important historical events. Now an exhibit hall, it houses a model of the hall under construction and displays the carpentry tools used at the time.

☞ To Visit: Carpenters' Hall

Carpenters' Hall
320 Chestnut Street
Philadelphia, PA 19106
215-925-0167
Hours: Tuesday-Sunday, 10 A.M.-4 P.M.
Admission free.

BETTING IS OLD BUSINESS

Lottery fever is not new. The Continental Congress held the first national lottery on April 10, 1777, for the same reason there are lotteries today—the state needed money! Treasury bank notes were the prizes, payable at the end of five years. (Imagine waiting five years for the payoff today!) Proceeds from the sale of lottery tickets were used by Philadelphia's city council to remodel existing government buildings and construct new ones. The council reasoned that smart-looking government buildings would entice the federal government to establish Philadelphia as the permanent capital of the young nation. Alas, it didn't work.

MORE FIRSTS

☆ The **first patent for rubber** was granted to Jacob Frederick Hummel on April 29, 1813, for a "varnish of elastic gum to render waterproof" shoes and other objects.

☆ Until 1784, seed was imported from Europe. David Landreth had a better idea, and established the **first seed business** in an area of the city that's now 12th and Market Streets. Years later, the D. Landreth Seed Company was absorbed by the Robert Buist Company, founded in Philadelphia in 1828. Although the Buist Company is long gone, Robert Buist is known for his writings about the green rose and for naming the poinsettia.

☆ The **first and oldest advertising agency** in the United States is N.W. Ayer & Son, established in Philadelphia in 1869. It moved its operations to New York in 1973.

☆ W. E. Kreusi taught the **first course in marketing** at the University of Pennsylvania in 1904.

☆ Progress Plaza, established in 1971, was the **first shopping center owned and operated by black businessmen**. Part of the Reverend Leon Sullivan's initiative to move Philadelphia's blacks into the financial mainstream, the shopping center on North Broad Street still exists and is a thriving enterprise.

School Days

The first Quaker grammar school was established in Philadelphia in 1689 by the Society of Friends, in response to a charge by William Penn. George Keith headed the school, and one of the conditions of his employment was that he agree to teach poor children at no cost. They were taught for free, but separately from paying students. This school, the William Penn Charter School, has been in existence for more than 300 years, and to this day continues its commitment to Quaker spiritual and educational philosophies.

THE EARLIEST PUBLIC SCHOOLING

Before the William Penn Charter School opened, and only five years after the city was settled, Enoch Flower ran a rather haphazard effort to educate Philadelphia's youngsters—with no established school taxes, board of education, referenda, or other public input. He was paid modest fees by parents to educate their children. These fees depended upon what he taught his students: four shillings for reading, six shillings for reading and writing, and eight shillings for reading, writing, and arithmetic.

William Penn Charter School, the first school in the nation, as its Chestnut Hill campus looks today. *Courtesy of William Penn Charter School*

PUBLIC AND PRIVATE EDUCATION THRIVE

Benjamin Franklin's great-grandson, Dr. Alexander Dallas Bache, established Central High School on Juniper Street, east of Penn Square, in 1836. It was the first high school in the nation to confer bachelor of arts degrees upon its graduates. Qualified students were—and still are—granted the degree upon the approval of the state legislature. In its heydey, the four-year school offered superior courses, and its astronomical observatory featured telescopes better than those at Harvard and the United States Naval Observatory.

From time to time, the state legislature tries to rescind the right of the school to grant college degrees, arguing that the degree does not have the same status it did back when graduates could go directly into a professional school from Central. But whenever the proposal to rescind is introduced, the alumni rise up in protest and have so far succeeded in maintaining Central's right to grant bachelor's degrees.

Until 1984, Central High was restricted to males. The first coed class had seven women in it; now they make up 53 percent of the school population. Central boasts many distinguished graduates, among them James M. Forsyth, rear admiral, U.S. Navy; Cyrus Adler, world-renowned Orientalist; Dr. Albert C. Barnes, philanthropist and art collector; Philip Rosenbach, bibliophile; and artist Thomas Eakins.

GIRARD COLLEGE: WHERE EDUCATION AND ALTRUISM MEET

The one-eyed French immigrant Stephen Girard arrived in Philadelphia in 1776, already a shipowner at age 26, with a talent for making money. Today we'd probably call him a venture capitalist. He was instrumental in developing the Port of Philadelphia, and he bailed out the federal government in the War of 1812. When Girard died in 1831, he left an estate unheard of in those days: $6 million in cash and real estate, plus bequests to fund improvements to Philadelphia and for public use in Pennsylvania and New Orleans. (Today, his fortune would be the equivalent of $225 million.) Part of his bequest to Philadelphia was to educate "poor male white orphans" in the first such school in the country. Girard College, not actually a college but rather an elementary school and a high school, was founded in 1848 for that purpose. At its opening on January 1, 100 students were enrolled, and by October of the same year another 100 had been admitted.

GIRARD'S LEGACY

"To rest is to rust" was Stephen Girard's motto, and the school that bears his name is based on that maxim.

Stephen Girard—entrepreneur, industrial magnate, philanthropist, and founder of Girard College. *Courtesy of the Stephen Girard Collection of Girard College*

CHALLENGED BY LAWSUITS

Stephen Girard's relatives, angry at being cut out of his will, hired Daniel Webster to bring suit against his estate. But after a 13-year battle, the will was upheld by the U.S. Supreme Court. Then in 1968, 137 years after his death, Girard's bequest was again in dispute, now over the school's white-male-only policy. This time the court ruled against Girard, and the school was opened to boys of any race. In 1984, the school voluntarily began admitting female students. Today, its enrollment is about 80 percent African American.

Girard College educates children ages 6 through 18, and it offers a full college preparatory program in the high school. It's also a residential facility, so the trustees and the administration are responsible for the personal as well as the academic welfare of the students. Girard's intent in establishing the school was to provide fatherless boys with the kind of nurturing and moral environment that other children could expect from a traditional home life. He stipulated that the boys not be influenced in any doctrinaire way, and although Girard was a religious person himself, clergymen were barred from participation in the college.

In addition to educating children, the school acts as a sort of memorial to Girard, housing a museum with much of his furniture and personal effects. His remains rest in a stone coffin at the entrance of Founder's Hall. His vision for the city and his compassion for needy, orphaned children remain his legacy.

A UNIVERSITY IS BORN

Benjamin Franklin's pamphlet "Proposals Relating to the Education of Youth in Pennsylvania," written in 1749, was the genesis of the University of Pennsylvania, the first non-sectarian institution of higher learning in the colonies. The university was originally located on Fourth Street, because Franklin wanted the school to be surrounded by an orchard and green meadows. This environment is a far cry from the bustle and sounds—the construction noises and the seemingly constant sirens—that today encroach upon the Penn campus, which is in West Philadelphia and extends from 34th Street to beyond 40th, from South Street to Market, and beyond.

The school's curriculum was the first liberal arts program in the country. In compliance with Franklin's principles of education, and unlike college curricula in England that concentrated only on the classics, it integrated traditional classic subjects with physics, chemistry, natural history, mathematics, economics, and modern languages. The university traces its origins

An early drawing of the College of Philadelphia, which merged with the University of the State of Pennsylvania to become the University of Pennsylvania. *Courtesy of the University of Pennsylvania Archives and Records Center*

to a tuition-free school founded in 1740 to instruct young men in the professions and in modern languages. In 1751, Franklin opened his academy in the charity school's building, and in 1755 the academy and the charity school were chartered as the College of Philadelphia. Local money supported the school, but so did contributions from England, and this English support created turmoil among the trustees during the American Revolution because many of them were loyalists. In 1779, the Pennsylvania Assembly declared the College's charter void and the property was deeded to a new group of trustees, who were mandated to found a new institution called the University of the State of Pennsylvania.

Never Say Die

But the old College refused to close its doors, and continued limping along until the Assembly realized that the newly constituted university was inadequate in fulfilling its academic mandate. The act of 1779 was revoked and the property returned to the College of Philadelphia. The University was just as tenacious as the College, and it also remained in place! For a few years, the College and the University coexisted, neither one growing or accomplishing much. In 1791 the legislature created a union of the two, new trustees were selected, and the University of Pennsylvania, as the combined schools were called, continued to struggle until new buildings were purchased and Franklin's dream of higher education was realized.

STUDENTS GET IN THE ACT

The first U.S. university had the first student union in the nation. Houston Hall was built in 1896 and enlarged in 1929. It boasted its own swimming pool, affectionately referred to as the Houston Club Tank.

EVERYWHERE A MUSEUM

In a small, rented second-floor room, a Philadelphia chemist displayed a dozen stuffed birds and a few jars of reptiles and formed a small society to discuss "the operations of nature." From these humble beginnings, the Philadelphia Academy of Natural Sciences was established in 1812 as a pioneering scientific institution "for the encouragement and cultivation of the sciences, and the advancement of useful learning." It's the oldest natural history institution in the Western Hemisphere. Many expeditions have been undertaken under its auspices, including the Western wilderness, the Arctic, Central America, Africa, and Asia. An 1868 exhibit boasted the first dinosaur skeleton ever on public display.

☞ *To Visit: Academy of Natural Sciences*

Academy of Natural Sciences
19th Street and Benjamin Franklin Parkway
Philadelphia, PA 19103
215-299-1000
Hours: Monday-Friday, 10 A.M.-4:30 P.M.; weekends and holidays,
10 A.M.-5 P.M.
Closed Christmas and New Year's Day.
Admission charged.

MUMMIES AND MEMENTOS

Mummies in Philadelphia? You bet. They're resting peacefully for all to see at the University of Pennsylvania Museum of Archaeology and Anthropology, an institution dedicated to understanding the heritage of humankind. The museum has many archaeological and anthropological firsts to its credit. Founded in 1887 as the Archaeological Association, it became the University Museum in 1892. The Babylonian Expedition of 1888 was a real coup for the museum: when the committee in charge of this expedition discovered it was unable to prevent illicit excavations in this area, it bought two private collections of antiquities for less money than the actual expedition would have cost. Now, the museum houses the greatest gathering of Babylonian and Assyrian relics that exists anywhere.

Digs in Ancient Cities

Perhaps the museum's most renowned excavation took place in 1889–90 at Nippur, ancient city of Sumerians and Akkadians. Today it is known as Iraq. This was the first expedition of its kind to the Middle East. In 1931, the museum was the first in the country to excavate in Iran. Another

The red granite sphinx of Rameses II holds court in the Egyptian Wing of the University of Pennsylvania Museum of Archaeology and Anthropology. *Courtesy of University of Pennsylvania Museum Photographic Archives*

notable first was the development of underwater archaeology. In the 1960s, the museum designed and built a two-man submarine to embark on underwater explorations. Until that time, archaeologists had had to rely on treasure hunters to locate and acquire valuables from old shipwrecks. The museum administration decided these underwater treasures should be acquired by academic institutions for study and preservation. The first such enterprise was off the coast of Turkey, where a Bronze Age wreck was located. Under the leadership of George Bass, the expedition acquired pottery and ingots, and developed sound recording and excavation techniques for underwater exploration.

The museum has sent more than 350 archaeological and anthropological expeditions to the inhabited continents of the world.

☞ *To Visit: University of Pennsylvania Museum of Archaeology and Anthropology*

University of Pennsylvania Museum
33rd and Spruce Streets
Philadelphia, PA 19104
215-898-4000
Hours: Tuesday-Saturday, 10 A.M.- 4:30 P.M.; Sundays, 1-5 P.M.
Closed holidays and summer Sundays (from Memorial Day through Labor Day).
Admission charged.

READING IS EVERYTHING

Who better than a publisher, writer, inventor, and all-around genius to conceive the idea of a public library? Thanks go to Benjamin Franklin, who, with a group of friends, formed the Library Company of Philadelphia, the first library open to the public (albeit the paying public) on this side of the Atlantic, and the nation's oldest cultural organization.

It started as a subscription library, which meant that people paid a small fee to join, or "subscribe," and use its facilities. Books were initially purchased with annual contributions made by each shareholder. None of the founders deemed themselves sufficiently erudite to select the books, so they asked James Logan, "a gentleman of universal learning and the best judge of books in these parts," to make the selections and purchase them from England. Any "civil gentleman" could come in and read the books, but, much like today's library card holders, only subscribers could take them home.

The library became the de facto Library of Congress, and it remained the largest public library in North America through the middle of the 19th century. Today, it is virtually the only colonial library that remains intact. The library provides exhibitions and public programs of colloquia, lectures, and publications. Its facilities are open to the public.

☞ *To Visit: Library Company of Philadelphia*

Library Company of Philadelphia
1314 Locust Street
Philadelphia, PA 19107-5698
215-546-3181
Hours: Reading Room, Print Room, and Exhibition Gallery: weekdays,
9 A.M.-4:45 P.M.; Print Room: appointments recommended.
Closed holidays.
Admission free.

FIRST COPY OF THE DECLARATION OF INDEPENDENCE

A copy of the first printed edition of the Declaration of Independence was discovered, among many other finds, at Leary's bookstore on Ninth Street, south of Market. Leary's was a Philadelphia landmark for more than a century, and is sorely missed by many book lovers. The oldest bookstore in the country, it closed on November 20, 1969, after 132 years of operation. On the New Year's Eve following its closing, a customer sorting books from the store found a copy of the first printed edition of the Declaration of Independence in the pages of an old scrapbook. The "broadsides" were set in type by Philadelphia printer John Dunlop the evening of July 4, 1776, just hours after the Declaration was approved. This copy was sold at auction for $404,000. (Either 7 or 21 copies still exist, depending on whom you talk to.)

TO INQUIRE IS TO KNOW

Benjamin Franklin sought to improve the intellectual quality not only of Philadelphia but of himself as well. In 1743, when he was 21, he organized the Junto, a society whose purpose was "for mutual improvement . . . for promoting useful knowledge among the British plantations in America"— to connect the aspiring science of the New World with the science of the

Old. The members met in a tavern and asked themselves questions such as "Is there any essential difference between the electric fluid and elementary fire?" Philosophical as well as scientific issues were fodder for this intellectual salon. The club remained in its intellectual pursuit until 1766, when it renamed itself the American Society for promoting and propagating Useful Knowledge. Three years later it united with the Philosophical Society. Franklin was the first president, succeeded by famous Philadelphia astronomer David Rittenhouse.

Philosophy Meets Science

The first momentous task undertaken by the American Philosophical Society was in 1769, when it embarked upon the observation of the transit of Venus. Not one for terseness, the society's early mandate was to pursue "all philosophical Experiments that let Light into the Nature of Things, tend to increase the Power of Man over Matter, and multiply the Convenience or

Benjamin Franklin's battery of Leyden jars, primitive but instrumental in his electrical experiments. *Courtesy of the American Philosophical Society*

Pleasures of Life." Most founders of the republic were members, including George Washington, John Adams, Thomas Jefferson, Alexander Hamilton, Thomas Paine, Benjamin Rush, James Madison, and John Marshall. Foreigners were not excluded; the Marquis de Lafayette, Baron Friedrich von Steuben, and Polish revolutionary leader Thaddeus Kosciusko were welcomed to the ranks. Through the discussions and interests of the society, Jefferson designed a model plough, Franklin pursued an interest in rice, and the Pennsylvania Assembly gave the society £1,000 to plant mulberry trees for silkworms, imported to the States, to feed on.

At first the society investigated issues considered scientific and technological. Today, it includes research in jurisprudence, clinical medicine, North American Indians, the history of science, and other contemporary issues. The society's library houses more than 180,000 volumes and periodicals, six million manuscripts, and thousands of maps and prints. The library hosts many scholarly conferences and seminars and is a major national center for research in the histories of science, medicine, and technology.

☞ To Visit: American Philosophical Society Library

American Philosophical Society Library
105 South Fifth Street
Philadelphia, PA 19106
215-440-3400
Hours: Monday-Friday, 9 A.M.-5 P.M.
Closed holidays.
Admission free.

FROM OUR HEARTS TO THE HEAVENS

The Franklin Institute, founded in 1824 for the promotion of mechanical and scientific studies, has come a long way. Its modest beginnings featured a group of young men who offered classes in architecture, mechanical drawing, mathematics, and modern languages. It is the oldest institution of its kind.

Past, Present, and Future Meet

The historic pieces at the institute include Benjamin Franklin's printing press and his original electrical apparatus. But relics of the past are just a part of what can be found there. The institute has grown with the times. From Matthias Baldwin's first locomotive to sophisticated interactive computer retrieval systems, from a model of the inside of the heart to the latest computer games, the Franklin Institute is a treasure house of scientific discoveries and adventure.

The original building was on Seventh Street, south of Market, and remained there for a century before moving to its present location on the Benjamin Franklin Parkway. The institute, true to its original mission, combines the search for scientific truth with examples of its practical application. Exhibits range from the history of electricity to complicated robotics. One of the most vivid memories of children who visit the Franklin Institute is of walking through the giant model of the human heart, touching its chambers and arteries and hearing its steady "thump, thump" beat.

☞ To Visit: The Franklin Institute Science Museum

The Franklin Institute Science Museum
20th Street and Benjamin Franklin Parkway
Philadelphia, PA 19103
215-448-1200
Hours: Daily, 9:30 A.M.-5 P.M.
Admission charged.

OUR COUNTRY'S FIRST ART MUSEUM

Charles Willson Peale founded the Pennsylvania Academy of the Fine Arts in 1805, with the help of 71 prominent Philadelphians who shared his vision. They created this nation's first art museum and school of fine arts. Masterpieces of American art have graced its galleries since its founding.

Gems of American Painting

The original academy, which was on the north side of Chestnut Street between 10th and 11th Streets, charged 25 cents for admission. A permanent collection was established, buoyed by exhibitions of new and well-known artists. The academy's student enrollment grew, as did the size of its exhibitions, making a new facility necessary. The result is the present building, a design marvel by architects Frank Furness and George Hewitt. It was dedicated on April 22, 1876.

Today, the variety of exhibitions reflect a variety of trends in American painting and sculpture. The exhibits for 1998, for example, ranged from works by landscape painter April Gornik to pop abstraction that featured the work of pop artists and minimalists like Jasper Johns, Roy Lichtenstein, Andy Warhol, and Robert Rauschenberg, as well as the work of recent academy graduates.

☞ To Visit: Pennsylvania Academy of the Fine Arts

Pennsylvania Academy of the Fine Arts
Museum of American Art
118 North Broad Street
Philadelphia, PA 19102
215-972-7600
Gallery hours: Monday-Saturday, 10 A.M.-5 P.M.; Sunday, 11 A.M.-5 P.M.
Admission charged.

THE PHILADELPHIA MUSEUM OF ART: A DRAWING CARD

The Philadelphia Museum of Art has succeeded in bringing the first retrospectives of the work of artists like Pablo Picasso, Henri Matisse, and Jan van Eyck, as well as photographer Robert Capra, not only to Philadelphia but to the nation. Visitors flock here from many states, and for its most popular exhibits, the museum issues timed tickets to manage the crowds.

The museum was founded in 1876, in conjunction with the Centennial Exhibition of that year. Three years before the Centennial, the Pennsylvania legislature authorized the construction of a permanent, fireproof building to serve as the art gallery of the exposition. This was Memorial Hall, and it remained in Fairmount Park as a museum of art and industry "for the improvement and enjoyment of the people of the Commonwealth." It is the one building still standing from the 1876 Centennial.

As permanent collections grew, plans were made for the construction of a new building on the site of a former reservoir in Fairmount Park. Building was to commence in 1907, but it was delayed until 1919. The design was for a large neoclassical temple. The two side wings were constructed first, but completion of the central hall joining them had to wait; the Depression made it impossible to get needed federal, city, and private funds. Today the museum houses more than 300,000 works of art.

THOSE FAMOUS STEPS

The dramatic entrance, with its fountains, Greek facade, and statuary, was made most famous by the movie *Rocky*, when actor Sylvester Stallone, who grew up in Philadelphia, raced up the front steps to train for the big fight.

☞ *To Visit: Philadelphia Museum of Art*

Philadelphia Museum of Art
26th Street and Benjamin Franklin Parkway
Philadelphia, PA 19101
215-763-8100
Hours: Tuesday and Thursday-Sunday, 10 A.M.-5 P.M.; Wednesday,
10 A.M.-8:45 P.M.
Closed major holidays.
Admission charged.

ART SCHOOL FOR WOMEN

The first industrial arts school for women, the Philadelphia School of Design for Women, was started in 1848 by philanthropist Sarah Worthington King Peter. She wanted to provide women with an education that would give them self-assurance and confidence in the profession of textile design. Until that time, most wallpapers, floor coverings, upholstery, and textiles, as well as lithographs and wood engravings, had to be imported from overseas. Peter believed that women were an untapped resource and could be trained to create American-made interior design furnishings.

THE PHILADELPHIA TEN

A 1998 exhibit at Moore College of Art & Design, celebrating the school's role in training women for careers in art, featured "The Philadelphia Ten," a female art group that existed for more than 25 years before the end of World War II. Nine of these women, all professional painters and sculptors, were graduates of the Philadelphia School of Design for Women.

Edith Lucile Howard, one of the original Philadelphia Ten painters, graduated from the Philadelphia School of Design for Women in 1908. She is pictured painting at the Grand Canyon around 1926. *Courtesy of Moore College of Art & Design*

Peter asked the board of managers of the Franklin Institute to help raise funds for the school, which would offer "needy and deserving women" drawing lessons and design training. After a few years, the school continued on its own and purchased the Gaul-Forrest Mansion, at 1346 North Broad Street, in 1880. This later became Moore College of Art & Design. In 1931, the school was approved by the state to grant Bachelor of Science in Art Education degrees, and it became the first independent art school in the United States to grant a degree of any kind.

KIDS ARE FIRST, TOO

Duck through a doorway, part a curtain, and come out the other side a clown! That's what kids love about the Please Touch Museum. Secret corners are filled with costumes to cater to flights of imagination. Mirrors show you what you can be when you smear your face with makeup. Exhibit areas offer the work of Maurice Sendak. There's also a well-stocked, pint-size

Having fun in a museum means costumes, games, and "let's pretend." This happens every day at the Please Touch Museum. *Courtesy of the Please Touch Museum*

supermarket, a science park, and a miniature television studio that provides an opportunity for the young to experiment with live sound and picture.

Founded in 1976 by a group of educators, artists, and parents, and guided by Montessori educator Portia Sperr, the Please Touch Museum was the first museum in the nation built specifically for children ages one to seven. The museum's goal was to stimulate the curiosity and understanding of children through hands-on exhibits, programs, and collections that encourage adult/child interaction in the arts, sciences, and humanities. The idea worked so well that it was quickly imitated, and now there are several hands-on children's museums throughout the country.

☞ To Visit: Please Touch Museum

Please Touch Museum
210 North 21st Street
Philadelphia, PA 19103
215-963-0667
Hours: Daily, 9 A.M.-4:30 P.M.; July 1-Labor Day, 9 A.M.-6 P.M.
Closed Thanksgiving, Christmas, and New Year's Day.
Admission charged.

The Curtis Institute of Music, founded in 1928, was the first tuition-free conservatory in the country. The institute was responsible for several musical firsts, such as premiering the composition "Dover Beach," by Samuel Barber, in 1932 and Gian-Carlo Menotti's opera *Amelia al Ballo* in 1937. The Symphony Orchestra of Curtis plays several concerts a year at the Academy of Music, showcasing the talents of major soloists and conductors. It was the first conservatory orchestra to release a recording under a major label. With Andre Previn conducting, the CD features composer Vaughan Williams' "Fantasies on a Theme by Thomas Tallis" and his Symphony No. 5, as well as the first recording of Previn's "Reflections." Curtis graduates often become big names in the classical music world. And they make up nearly half the members of the Philadelphia Orchestra.

They start them early at Settlement Music School. These little ones are students at the Children's Music Workshop, an introductory course in music offered at all locations.
Courtesy of Nick Kelsh and Settlement Music School

Music Lessons for Five Cents

When Settlement Music School was founded in 1908 in the neighborhood settlement house in the Southwark section of Philadelphia, it was the only place around that offered very inexpensive music lessons—they were five cents each. The school grew rapidly, and today it is the largest community school of music in the nation, with branches throughout the city. The school founded the National Guild of Community Schools of the Arts and became its first member. Now, about 9,000 students, ranging from three-year-olds to senior citizens, attend each year. Some notable alumni include Chubby Checker, Buddy Greco, and Mario Lanza, in addition to members of major symphonies, opera companies, and, of course, the Philadelphia Orchestra.

MORE FIRSTS

☆ The **first formal school for African American children**, the Benezet School, was established in Philadelphia in 1750 by Anthony Benezet. He began to conduct classes in his home for African American children, and he continued to do so for the next 20 years. In 1754, concerned about education for females, Benezet started a school for girls. The curriculum included Latin, Greek, and needlework.

☆ The **first American Sunday School Union** was founded in Philadelphia in 1824 to "circulate moral and religious publications in every part of the land."

☆ The **first national teachers convention** met in the Hall of the Controllers of the Public Schools on August 26, 1857, to organize the National Teachers Association. Some years later the name was changed to the National Education Association.

☆ Maimonides College, founded in this city in 1867, was the **first rabbinic school**, the first Jewish institute of higher learning in the United States.

☆ The **oldest art club in the country**, the Philadelphia Sketch Club, was organized here about 1868.

Reading, Writing, Listening, and Watching

MAGAZINES ARE EVERYWHERE

In colonial days, printers were the editors and publishers of their time. Because they had the means of production (limited as it was), these early journalists were in the unique position of being able to print and distribute their opinions.

The Bradford and Franklin families were the leading printers and the editors and publishers of the day. And in 1741, William Bradford published the first magazine in America: *The American Magazine, or a Monthly View of the Political State of the British Colonies.* John Webbe was the editor. This periodical made its first appearance on February 13, which meant that it preceded by about three days Benjamin Franklin's magazine, *The General Magazine and Historical Chronicle for All the British Plantations in America.* Although it was not his style to be bested, Franklin was runner-up this time. But Bradford's success was short-lived; his magazine lasted only about three months.

Old Ben never gave up on publishing ventures, and on May 6, 1782, he published the first German newspaper, *Die Philadelphische Zeitung.* Its success was even briefer than Bradford's: only two issues were ever published!

Godey's Lady's Book

Magazines grew to suit every taste, and the first successful women's magazine, *Godey's Lady's Book,* was published in Philadelphia in 1829 by

COMICS

The first comic weekly was *The John Donkey*, published by G.B. Zieber & Company and edited by Thomas Dunn English and George G. Foster. Sixteen pages sold for six cents a copy; even so, it lasted only from January to October of 1848.

Louis A. Godey, based on Sixth Street above Chestnut. Before the Civil War, this magazine surpassed the circulation of any other publication. The covers surely didn't promise articles like "How to Slim Your Hips in 30 Days." But fashion was always of interest, and *Godey's* featured pages of the latest clothing styles. The magazine's editor was Sarah Josepha Buell Hale (reputed author of "Mary Had a Little Lamb").

Hale, a widow with five children, was a novelist who was to become the most influential voice for women in America in her time. She worked for and wrote about the need for better education and opportunities for women, improved sanitation, and better medicine. She also helped found Vassar College. By the time of her death in 1879, she had written two dozen books.

Women's Issues and Interests

Godey's Lady's Book featured color fashion prints, now sought-after collectibles. In 1849, editor Hale boasted that the magazine published 916 pages and 281 engravings that year, and each issue featured a piece of music, needlework patterns, and "always moral and instructive" reading matter. There were articles such as "The Country Housewife," "Women of the Revolution," "A Nervous Wife, and how she was Cured," "Cruelty to Women," "Coffee, its History and Cultivation," "Sunday Evenings at

Home," and many others that reflected the issues of the time, especially for women.

ALL THE NEWS THAT FITS

The Pennsylvania Gazette was bought by Benjamin Franklin from Samuel Keimer, who had started the paper in 1728. Its original name was *The Universal Instructor in all Arts and Sciences: and Pennsylvania Gazette.*

FREE ADVERTISING

Ever the entrepreneur, Benjamin Franklin used the pages of his newspaper, *The Pennsylvania Gazette*, to report on the success of his lightning rod and give instructions on its use.

Benjamin Franklin drew this divided serpent, the first cartoon to appear in an American newspaper, telling the separate colonies that just as a segmented snake can reunite its parts, they'd better join together or die.

The political cartoon has been a standard for a long time, first appearing in this city in 1754 in *The Pennsylvania Gazette* to spoof local political battles. The artist: Benjamin Franklin. To support his proposal of a "Plan of Union" for the colonies, he drew a segmented serpent, divided into eight parts, with the caption "Join or Die." It appeared in the paper on May 9 and was quickly reprinted in virtually every newspaper published at that time.

The newspaper *The North American* was founded in 1839, and because it had bought out *The Pennsylvania Gazette,* it felt it had the right to call itself "the oldest newspaper in the country." In 1898, *The North American* was purchased by department store magnate John Wanamaker. Newspapers change hands frequently, and this one was no exception. The last edition was published in 1925, when it was bought by Cyrus Curtis' *Public Ledger.* In 1933, the *Philadelphia Inquirer* absorbed the *Public Ledger,* making the *Inquirer* a descendant of the first newspaper in the nation.

News Every Day

These earliest papers weren't published daily. The first daily in the United States, *The Pennsylvania Packet* (initially named *The Pennsylvania Packet and*

PAPERS FOR A PENNY

The first penny newspaper, *The Cent,* was published in 1830 by Dr. Christopher Columbus Conwell, at Second and Dock Streets. The Penny Press (whose newspapers sold for one penny) came into existence in the 1830s. The bargain rate was due in part to new technologies that gave us cheaper newsprint—and also to the growing market, as more and more people learned to read.

Daily Advertiser), was started by John Dunlop and David C. Claypoole. First issued on October 28, 1771, as a weekly, *The Pennsylvania Packet* became the first daily newspaper in the nation on Tuesday, September 21, 1784.

THE PEN AND PENCIL CLUB

Pencil in hand, green eyeshade, cigarette dangling, hat perched low on the forehead—that's the picture we have of the old-time newspaper reporters. They wanted to talk shop after work as well as at their desks, so Philadelphia journalists formed the first news reporters association, the Pen and Pencil Club, the oldest newswriters' organization in the country—and still in existence.

BOOK BEGINNINGS

Although not the first publishing house in the country, Lea & Febiger is the oldest still in existence. Owned by members of the original family, the company is responsible for many publishing firsts.

Founder Mathew Carey, who was interested in printing and publishing as a youth, learned much of his trade at the feet of the master, Benjamin Franklin, when he worked at Franklin's print shop in France. Carey arrived in Philadelphia in 1782, and with some funds borrowed from the Marquis de Lafayette, did what many publishers did: he established a newspaper, *Carey's Pennsylvania Evening Herald*. And the first issue, printed on January 25, 1785, was the beginning of his company. He published the debates of the House of Assembly from notes he took himself, using a shorthand process of his own creation.

Catalogs, Pamphlets, and More

Carey's firm, under the management of his son, Henry, published the country's first gift annual, *The Atlantic Souvenir*. An immediate success, the catalog featured illustrations using new printing techniques—lithography, engraving, and mezzotint.

Carey was more than a publisher. An avid pamphleteer, he also began the first publishers' trade association and founded both the Hibernian Society and the first Sunday School Association in the United States. He was also something of a historian. He published Parson Mason Locke Weems' *Life of Washington*, the book that gave us the cherry tree story.

ALL THE NEWS THAT'S FIT TO PRINT

What made all these newspapers, books, and magazines possible was, of course, type. The first type foundry, imported from Germany, was permanently established by Christopher Sauer of Germantown, a clockmaker, in 1771. The first Bible printed in this country, which was in German, came from Sauer's press. The third edition of Sauer's Bible was a casualty of the Revolution; when British soldiers found it in his loft, they used it to make musket wadding.

How Printing Happens

George E. Clymer of Philadelphia invented America's first "improved" printing press. This was an iron hand printing press that featured a combination of compound levers to apply the pressure needed to press the type onto paper. He called it the Columbian Press, and it addressed some of the shortcomings of this country's first printing press, which was constructed in Philadelphia by Adam Ramage in 1795 and used a screw to apply the needed pressure.

RELIGIOUS PUBLISHING

The *Religious Remembrancer*, the first religious weekly newspaper, was issued in Philadelphia by John Welwood Scott in 1813. About 25 years later, the name was changed to *The Christian Observer*, which is still in print today. Scott was a ruling elder of the Pine Street Presbyterian Church. After 10 years in publishing, he entered the ministry and the paper passed into the hands of another Philadelphia family.

An English Bible

The first Bible in English, issued in two volumes, was produced by Robert Aitken, a Philadelphia printer, in 1782. This note appears in Aitken's handwriting on the back of the title page of the first volume (which is now in the British Museum):

> The first copy of the first edition of the Bible ever printed in America in the English language, is presented to Ebenezer Hazard, Esq., by the Editor.

Jewish Book Publishing

The Jewish Publication Society of America was co-founded by Judge Mayer Sulzberger. It was the first publishing company to focus specifically on theological texts and secular matters of Jewish interest.

The society was organized in 1845 at the urging of Isaac Leeser, the publisher of a monthly periodical, *The Occident and American Jewish Advocate*. Abraham Hart, a Philadelphia publisher from the firm of Carey & Hart (which issued the first edition of *Davy Crockett* and the first Thackeray novel, *Yellowplush Correspondence,* in 1838) agreed to serve as the first president of the society.

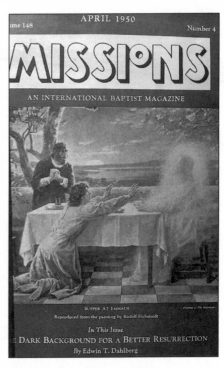

Two covers, one from 1925 and the other from 1950, reflect the publication *Missions*, published by the Baptist Church of America. *Courtesy of American Baptist Churches USA*

FOR THE BLIND

In January 1837 the first magazine for the blind, *Student's Magazine, a Periodical for the Blind*, was issued by the Pennsylvania Institution for the Instruction of the Blind—located in Philadelphia—using embossed, raised capital letters. In 1890, Edward E. Allen, superintendent of the Institution, adapted a dot system called New York Point to a modified Braille, allowing ordinary lowercase letters to be converted into capitals by prefixing two dots in the bottom of the preceding cell. Other schools for the blind soon followed this method, and in 1900 this system was named American Braille.

According to the archives of the Overbrook School for the Blind in Philadelphia, the Pennsylvania Institution published *The Book of Mark*, the first book in North America printed in embossing for the blind, in 1833, and the *Dictionary of the English language for the Blind*, the first dictionary for the blind (also in embossed print), in 1860.

BEFORE VOICE MAIL

The telephone was introduced to the world in 1876 at the Centennial Exhibition in Fairmount Park. Think of the primitive telephones that children make out of two cans and a long piece of string connecting them and you have a pretty good idea of what this early phone looked like. The instrument was quite crude—two cone-like shapes, attached to what resembled spools, and connected to each other by 500 feet of wire. The device sat for six weeks in the main building, unnoticed until a famous visitor discovered it.

The instrument had been sent to Philadelphia by Alexander Graham Bell, a little-known Boston elocution teacher who came to the exhibit on impulse. He hadn't been invited. Neither he nor his invention was given any attention until the emperor of Brazil, by chance, picked up the device and heard a voice from the other end of the wire, in another room. "My God," he shouted. "It talks!" Sir William Thomson, the foremost electrical scientist in the world at the time, was in the crowd and heard this exclamation.

Big Bells, Little Bells

Following this demonstration, when it was clear that Bell's telephone had enormous commercial possibilities, investors entered the picture and the Telephone Company of Philadelphia was formed. (Bell's name was not added until sometime later.)

Other companies, seeing the potential of Bell's invention, were eager to get into the telephone business. Soon after the Centennial demonstration, Daniel Connelly of Philadelphia, along with two partners, patented an automatic telephone system that featured a dial switching mechanism; however, it could accommodate only a few lines and so was not commercially applicable. The first switchboard was set up on the second floor at 1111 Chestnut Street, and the first telephone directory, which made its appearance in 1878, listed 25 names.

GRAY TRIES; BELL WINS

Elisha Gray, the inventor of the harmonic telegraph who worked on improving Morse's telegraph, was working on a telephone at the same time as Alexander Graham Bell, and the competition between them was bitter. They both exhibited at the Centennial: Gray his multiplex, which he called a "talking telegraph," and Bell his primitive telephone. Although the judges were amazed when Gray's multiplex received eight messages at once from New York, they awarded first prize for scientific achievement to Bell.

Competition for telephone business was fierce, especially between Bell's company and the Keystone Telephone Company, which was organized on November 12, 1902. These two rivals existed side by side, literally, for many years. Before telephones were commonplace in homes, people went to the corner drugstore to make their calls. And there, the Bell and Keystone phone booths stood next to each other. Children earned pocket money by hanging around the phones, and when they rang, running to whichever neighbor had a call. Their tip was usually five cents, the cost of a phone call.

Number, Please

The Commercial Exchange Building was the site of the country's first automatic telephone exchange, installed by Bell Telephone Company. The location had its own history: Originally, William Penn lived on the premises in a house built in 1687 with a then-unique slate roof, which led to its being called the Slate Roof House. The Slate Roof House had many distinguished residents after Penn, including James Logan, Governor James Hamilton, Revolutionary War general Charles Lee, and British general John Forbes. After the house was razed in 1867, the Commercial Exchange Building was erected on the site, but it had to be built twice because the first building was destroyed by fire the year after it was built. It was rebuilt in 1870.

The Keystone Telephone Company took over the building in 1903, but ultimately, when Bell absorbed Keystone, it assumed ownership of the building and installed the first automatic telephone exchange there.

The Slate Roof House, first the home of William Penn. After housing a number of famous Philadelphians, it became the Commercial Exchange Building. Eventually, the house was the headquarters of Bell Telephone Company.

People Start Talking

Long-distance telephone service began on March 31, 1877 (or, as some historians claim, April 1), when music played in Philadelphia was heard at Steinway Hall in New York City. It included Elisha Gray's "Transmission of Music by Telegraph," as well as some old favorites, like "The Last Rose of Summer," "Home, Sweet Home," and "Yankee Doodle." The music, heard over telephone wires, was transmitted from the office of the Western Union Telegraph Company at 10th and Chestnut Streets.

SKY TALK

Arthur Atwater Kent, a prominent Philadelphia manufacturer, had a radio telephone conversation with his wife from a dirigible on May 16, 1925. She was at the receiving end, in an automobile in Philadelphia. This was the first transmission of its kind, accomplished by means of a 300-foot-long wire trailing from the airship.

ARE YOU LISTENING?

The first experimental radio license was issued to St. Joseph's College in Philadelphia by the Department of Commerce on August 13, 1912, following the International Radio Convention and Radio Act. But radio waves were in the air before then: in 1910, Robert F. Miller of the United Wireless Telegraph Company won a company-sponsored radio contest for speed and accuracy using American Morse telegraphic code.

The Better to Hear You

The first stereophonic sound program required almost as much effort from the listener as from the broadcaster. On November 5, 1955, radio stations KYW and WFLN broadcast "Sounds of Tomorrow" simultaneously from the high-fidelity music show at the Benjamin Franklin Hotel. Listeners were told to tune in to KYW-AM and WFLN-FM simultaneously and arrange their sets approximately 12 feet apart with the same volume on each set. If all went well, stereophonic sound could be heard!

THE COUCH POTATO IS BORN

In 1934, the Stearns Auditorium of the Franklin Institute was the site of the first demonstration of electronic TV. Philo Farnsworth, a Utah farm boy, developed the basics of electronic television in the early 1920s. At that time, developers were using a primitive technology called scanning-disc schemes. (*The Random House Dictionary* defines a scanning disc as "a disc with a line of holes spiraling in from its edge, rotated in front of a surface so as to expose a small segment as each hole passes before it for transmitting or reproducing a picture.")

But Farnsworth persuaded investors to back him and his camera tubes and cathode ray tubes (CRTs). A camera tube is a CRT that converts an optical picture projected onto it into an electrical signal that can be transmitted. Then the CRT converts the electrical signal back into a picture. It's the camera tube that makes TV sets so deep and makes them take up so much shelf space. Previous demonstrations of television used either mechanical or hybrid systems. Farnsworth's creation was the first all-electronic system.

Let the Picture Begin

Farnsworth set up offices of the San Francisco Company, Television Laboratories, Ltd., in Chestnut Hill, a Philadelphia neighborhood. A mobile television system he built for display at the Chicago World's Fair was used for the demonstration at the Franklin Institute. After issuing licenses for the system to British and German companies, Farnsworth used the proceeds to establish his experimental television station, W3XPF, in Wyndmoor, Pennsylvania, just outside the city.

CELEBRATING TELEVISION

In January 1997, the Franklin Institute celebrated its part in the advancement of TV technology with a ceremony to introduce a new book and a video about the creation of television. The book, *Distant Vision*, was written by Philo Farnsworth's widow, Elma. The video, "Television: Big Dream, Small Screen," was shown in the Stearns Auditorium, site of the original demonstration, and on public television stations.

MORE FIRSTS

☆ In 1685, William Bradford published the **first book** in the colonies.

☆ The **first American type foundry** was established here in 1796 by Binney & Ronaldson.

☆ In 1804, the **first printing ink works** were established by Charles Eneu Johnson.

☆ Bass Otis, in 1819, created the **first American lithograph**, which appeared in the June issue of the *Philadelphia Analectic Magazine*. It was a portrait of the Reverend Abner Kneeland.

☆ In 1858, Hyman L. Lipman invented a **pencil with eraser**. The pencil had a groove at one end that held a glued-in piece of rubber eraser. Almost 40 years later, in 1895, Frederick E. Blaisdell invented a **paper pencil**, as well as a machine to manufacture his product, which was actually a paper-wrapped lead pencil. While it worked well technically, the writing public preferred something they could whittle, so it never took root.

☆ Philadelphian Leon Levy invented the **first engraving process that permitted newspapers to print photographs in halftone** (a black-and-white illustration in which light and dark shades are reproduced by means of small and large dots, used primarily in newspapers and magazines). Halftones first appeared in newspapers in 1871.

☆ The Lanston Monotype Manufacturing Company was founded here in 1892 by the inventor of the **monotype machine** (a mechanized typesetting system where the product is a galley of individual letters cast in lead type) and became the nation's major manufacturer of specialized publishing equipment.

☆ The **first "western" novel** was written by Philadelphian Owen Wister. *The Virginian* was published in 1902 and became a bestseller.

Is There a Doctor in the House?

In 1750, Dr. Thomas Bond appealed to "rich widows and other single women" for funds to establish a Quaker public mental hospital to provide for the "sick and distemperoid stranger." The first private mental institution had already been established in Philadelphia by the Quakers in 1709.

When they later proposed creating Pennsylvania Hospital, the Quakers mandated that a portion of the building be designated to house the insane. By 1841, Pennsylvania Hospital's department to care for the mentally ill had developed into the Pennsylvania Hospital for the Insane (later known as the Institute of Pennsylvania Hospital). However, during the hospital's early years, mentally ill patients were housed in basement rooms, subjected to harsh temperatures, and kept on display for paying oglers.

Think of it. No television, no movies, limited reading matter (limited literacy), and not much in the way of entertainment. What was a person to do? In colonial times, gawking at the insane was a form of recreation. This didn't begin as a fee-for-watching scheme, but evolved when hospital personnel, despite fences and doors, couldn't keep the curious from staring at, talking to, and teasing the inmates. Finally, in 1762, the hospital board decreed by inscription: "Persons who come out of curiosity to visit the house should pay a sum of money, a groat at least, for admittance."

Those deemed insane, but rich, had a different experience. They were often housed in another part of the hospital, segregated from other patients, and sometimes attended by personal servants. Among some familiar names who were housed in this way were Benjamin Rush's son, Charles Willson Peale's daughter, and Stephen Girard's wife.

Psychiatry Begins Here

Dr. Benjamin Rush, signer of the Declaration of Independence and surgeon-general of the Continental Army, is considered the father of American psychiatry. He was always concerned about the inadequacies of the treatment available to "mad people" and the way they were regarded. This led the Philadelphia Yearly Meeting to recommend that a separate asylum be established to treat Friends "deprived of their reason."

In 1817, ground was broken in Frankford for a facility that would address many of Rush's concerns. Known as Friends Asylum, it was one of the earliest hospitals in the country devoted to the care and treatment of the mentally ill.

BEFORE PROZAC

Around 1800, Dr. Benjamin Rush invented the "tranquilizing chair," a piece of furniture designed to comfort the unstable. Rush's likeness still appears as an emblem on the American Psychiatric Society's stationery and membership cards.

The likeness of Dr. Benjamin Rush, considered the father of American psychiatry, is used as a logo for the American Psychiatric Association and shown on stationery and all material sent out by the association.

Thomas Scattergood, a tanner by profession and a minister by faith, was the founding father of Friends Asylum. Not a happy man himself (his friends called him a "mournful prophet"), he visited a retreat in England that was designed to treat the mentally ill compassionately and humanely so that he could get ideas for improving the status of mental patients in the colonies. Scattergood made the proposal for a similar facility to the Philadelphia Meeting, and Friends Asylum was the result. Eventually, the name was changed to Friends Hospital.

Creating Calm

The Quakers were particularly interested in freeing that spark of "divine principle" they believed existed in every person. Land around the hospital included shaded walks, a stream, and a farm that patients worked to create a completely self-sufficient facility. Separation from the outside world, in a calm and wholesome environment, was meant to instill a sense of order and stability in troubled lives. No manacles, handcuffs, iron

Friends Hospital, circa 1840. The hospital was founded by the Religious Society of Friends to provide "moral treatment" to the mentally ill. The circular railway was installed in 1835 for the pleasure and recreation of patients. *Courtesy of Friends Hospital*

grates, or bars were used. Separate quarters for the violent, and light and airy rooms for quieter patients, helped reduce the feeling of confinement.

At that time, such civilized treatment of the mentally ill was unheard of. The hospital's construction, architecture, and emphasis on humane treatment received praise from medical professionals, and Friends Asylum attracted visitors from other parts of the country who came to learn more about its progressive methods. The hospital also inspired the building of other institutions with similar ideals.

Psychiatry Continues

Almost two centuries later, Philadelphia is still a leader in psychiatric pioneering. Dr. O. Spurgeon English studied medicine at Jefferson Medical College and graduated in 1924. He became a psychoanalyst and established the Department of Psychiatry at Temple University Hospital. His important contribution was as a proponent of and pioneer in the field of psychosomatic medicine, the concept that emotional stress can cause physical illness. In some ways this was a precursor to today's holistic medical practices that emphasize a mind-body approach to wellness. Dr. English was also responsible for spearheading the Philadelphia Psychoanalytic Institute, with its emphasis on interaction between patient and analyst.

TRAINING DOCTORS

The first medical school in the nation was established at the College of Philadelphia (later the University of Pennsylvania) by Dr. John Morgan in 1765. His speech "Discourse Upon the Institution of Medical Schools in America," delivered on May 30 of that year, formally opened the school. Morgan was not only the school's first medical professor, he was also the first such professor in the nation. Three years later, medical honors were conferred upon the first class, the first time such an event occurred in the colonies. In the same year, the first medical society was organized.

FIRST HOSPITAL

The gifts of an articulated human skeleton and a collection of anatomical models and drawings from Dr. John Fothergill of London helped start Pennsylvania Hospital, the first in the nation. The hospital was founded in 1751 by Benjamin Franklin and Dr. Thomas Bond. The hospital's original building, the Pine Building, is still in use. The basement housed the insane, the first floor was for men, the second for women, and the third housed servants and isolation cases of both sexes. The hospital was funded by donations from Quakers, other churches, and generous citizens. Even England contributed to its beginnings by passing an act of Parliament that turned over to the hospital all unclaimed funds remaining in the coffers of the Pennsylvania Land Company.

THE SURGICAL THEATER

Surgical procedures at Pennsylvania Hospital were performed in its surgical amphitheater from 1804 to 1868. Before doctors knew how to prevent the risk of infection during operations, surgery was limited to amputations, extractions, and aneurysm and hernia repairs.

Franklin was on the hospital's first board of managers, and he was elected president of the board in 1756. Franklin proposed, as he did for many of his pet organizations, that gold-lettered tin boxes that read "Charity for the Hospital" be placed in public buildings for donations.

A HOSPITAL FOR CHILDREN

Did doctors give sweets to children after a visit 100 years ago? We may not know, but we do know that pediatrics as a medical specialty began in the United States with the establishment in 1855 of the Children's Hospital of Philadelphia (familiarly known as CHOP). It was begun by Dr. Francis Lewis and two colleagues. Children's Hospital was the first in the United States to provide formal training in pediatrics.

Medical Breakthroughs

Concentrating on the medical treatment of children resulted in many firsts. The nursery incubator was invented by Dr. Charles C. Chapple at Children's Hospital in 1938. Later, it was patented under the name "Isolette Incubator," and used throughout the world. A pilot program developed at CHOP in 1962 ushered in the first neonatal intensive care unit in the nation. Initially, the unit was used when there were life-threatening surgical problems, but it eventually expanded to include many kinds of medical disorders.

CHOP Pioneers

The balloon catheter, in such common use now to enlarge heart openings and treat congenital heart diseases, was developed at CHOP in 1965 by Dr. William J. Rashkind, who is considered the father of intersternal cardiology. A home care program targeted exclusively to children, the first of its type in the country, was initiated in 1965 at Children's Hospital. The hospital was a pioneer in virus research in pediatrics, establishing the first virus diagnostic laboratory of any clinical department in the nation. It also developed plastic surgical techniques for repairing cleft lips and cleft palates.

Stop that coughing! You can, because whooping cough serum was developed at Children's Hospital in 1936. Eventually, the serum was manufactured and distributed in 48 states and 17 foreign countries. *Courtesy of Children's Hospital of Philadelphia*

MEDICINE MARCHES ON

Charles Christian Schieferdecker arrived in the city from Germany in 1839 to introduce hydropathy. In October 1846, he opened a "hydriatic institution" on the banks of the Schuylkill at Chestnut Street, where he guaranteed that his regimen could create a life span of 150 to 200 years. (Hey, Mr. Schieferdecker, where are you today?)

LEARNING HOW TO HEAL

The Hospital of the University of Pennsylvania, which opened its doors in the 1870s, was the first university teaching hospital in the nation. Before this, medical students were taught in medical schools that were unaffiliated with hospitals.

HUP Initiates Surgical Sleep

Giving a patient a big swig of whiskey was one way of making him insensible to pain, especially before amputations. Another was hypnosis! The services of traveling "mesmerizers" were used before and during surgical procedures. The process was called "animal magnetism," and the "anesthesiologists" used a combination of hypnosis and techniques with magnets during surgery, as well as afterward, for healing purposes. Once ether was invented, mesmerizers quickly disappeared. On March 30, 1842, ether was used for the first time during surgery by Dr. Crawford Long.

THE WISTAR INSTITUTE

The Wistar Institute of Anatomy and Biology, founded in 1892, was part of the University of Pennsylvania and the first university institute devoted solely to advanced study and research in anatomy and biology. Named after Dr. Caspar Wistar, who wrote the first American textbook on anatomy in 1811, the institute is the oldest independent medical research facility in the country.

After studying medicine in England, Wistar returned to Philadelphia in 1787 to practice. But medicine wasn't his only interest. In 1815, he succeeded his friend Thomas Jefferson as president of the American Philosophical Society.

The oldest independent medical research facility in the nation, the Wistar Institute of Anatomy and Biology was founded in 1892. *Courtesy of the Wistar Institute*

MEASLES BE GONE

German measles, or rubella, once a common and potentially serious child-hood illness, is rare these days because of the vaccine developed by Dr. Stanley A. Plotkin in 1963, in association with colleagues at the Wistar Institute of Anatomy and Biology.

Collections Aid in Research

Wistar had used wooden models of human anatomical features as teaching aids, along with dried and wax-injected human limbs and organs. He appointed a young physician, William Edmonds Horner, dean and professor of anatomy at Penn's medical school, to maintain his collection. Horner added other anatomical specimens to Wistar's and bequeathed the entire collection to the university, which established the Wistar and Horner Museum.

The collection, housed in Penn's Logan Hall in 1890, was left neglected and in sad shape after a bad fire. Wistar's great-nephew Isaac Jones Wistar never knew his great-uncle, but when he realized the importance of Caspar Wistar's collection, he encouraged the restoration of the museum and established an institution around it, independent but with strong links to the university.

ALL IN THE FAMILY

Isaac Jones Wistar was a young adventurer who became an attorney and a pillar of Philadelphia society. He was a Civil War general and served as president of the American Philosophical Society and the Academy of Natural Sciences.

Isaac Jones Wistar followed in the footsteps of his great-uncle, Caspar Wistar, as president of the American Philosophical Society.
Courtesy of the Wistar Institute

PETS NEED DOCTORS, TOO

People bring sick pets from all over the world to Penn's School of Veterinary Medicine. What they and Fido don't know is that this is the only school of veterinary medicine developed in association with a medical school; it was also the first vet school to have departments of nutrition and medical genetics.

The school was established in 1884 at the encouragement of the university's school of medicine, and it is firmly rooted in the medical sciences. It is one of the leading research, teaching, and clinical veterinary institutions in the world. In addition to its small animal hospital, the school operates the Laboratory for Marine Animal Health in Woods Hole, Massachusetts. The school's four-year program accepts about 109 students per year.

PROTECTING ANIMAL RIGHTS

The American Anti-Vivisection Society was organized in Philadelphia on February 23, 1883, by Caroline Earle White. Its main purpose was to restrict experiments on animals and prevent animal suffering. White was also an abolitionist and a children's rights activist working to abolish child labor.

SOME TEMPLE FIRSTS

Temple University Hospital is also no slouch in the department of medical firsts. In 1907, Dr. Wayne Babcock first used spinal anesthesia to eliminate pain during surgery. And in 1935, Dr. Temple Fay introduced hypothermia, reducing the body's temperature, during certain surgical procedures to slow down blood circulation and allow the heart and other vital organs to do less work.

The Temple University School of Medicine was the first in the country to admit and graduate a blind student. Dr. David Hartman graduated from Temple's medical school in 1976. He continued on to a residency in psychiatry at Penn, and now has a private psychiatric practice in Virginia.

BEHAVIOR MODIFICATION

Dr. Joseph Wolpe, a pioneer in new methods of treatment for emotional disorders, was the founder of behavior therapy, introduced in 1965 at Temple University Hospital. The objective of behavior therapy is to alter a patient's dangerous or undesirable behavior quickly and efficiently through conditioning techniques. The assumption is that what has been learned can be unlearned. This is unlike traditional psychotherapy, which strives to affect behavior through insight into and understanding of underlying or subconscious conflicts.

The father of behavior therapy, Dr. Joseph Wolpe, created the process that permits people to deal with uncomfortable behavior without undergoing the more traditional psychotherapy. *Courtesy of Temple University Health Sciences Center*

The Couch Makes Way

Wolpe, a South African psychologist, introduced such behavior modification techniques as systematic desensitization, assertiveness training, and aversion therapy to activate the patient to deal with his or her neurotic behavior by unlearning and changing the patterns that produced that behavior. Wolpe claimed that between 80 percent and 90 percent of his patients improved within six months of treatment. Although initially controversial because of his abandonment of Freudian techniques, which were very popular at the time, Wolpe's methods are now widely used to deal with phobias, addictions, psychosomatic disorders, stress, and other personal and social problems.

DOCTORS CONTINUE TO LEARN THEIR ART

In 1787, the College of Physicians and Surgeons was founded to promote medical education and advancement. It is the oldest existing medical society in the nation. John Redman was its founder and first president.

The imposing facade of the College of Physicians, at 19 South 22nd Street, unchanged since its completion in 1909. *Courtesy of the College of Physicians of Philadelphia*

WOMEN PHYSICIANS

Elizabeth Blackwell, the first woman in the nation to become a physician, came to the city in 1847 to obtain a medical education. She contacted each of the seven medical schools that existed in Philadelphia at the time. She was refused at all of them but was finally accepted at Geneva Medical College in Geneva, New York.

Blackwell's tenacity encouraged Philadelphia businessman William Mullen and others who believed in medical education for women to lobby in their behalf. Mullen was a true feminist who believed that women had been endowed "with the same intellectual constitution as man" and therefore had "the same right as man to intellectual culture and development." He also felt that women's nature was particularly suited to the study and practice of medicine. As a result of the efforts of Mullen and his supporters, on March 11, 1850, the state legislature granted a charter for the first college to educate women for the medical profession.

The first medical college for women had its beginnings in 1850 in two dark, rented lecture rooms. Its only teaching aids were papier-mâché models and one manikin. The school was originally named Female Medical College, then Women's Medical College, and after that, Medical College of Pennsylvania (MCP).

FIRST PHILADELPHIA FEMALE PHYSICIAN

Dr. Hannah Longshore was the first female physician in the city to open a private practice.

Protests at Graduation

"Forget you are women. . . . Remember you are physicians," advised Dr. Joseph Longshore in his valedictory address to the first graduating class of eight women in 1851. During the commencement exercises, police had to be called in to deal with protesters. Five hundred male medical students threatened to heckle at the ceremony and prevent the graduation from taking place because they believed these women lacked proper training and clinical experience to become physicians. The city dispatched 50 police officers to keep order, and there were no incidents. That night, dinner conversation at Philadelphia dining tables buzzed about the new "doctresses."

FIRST IN CANCER RESEARCH

The Hospital of Fox Chase Cancer Center, founded as American Oncologic Hospital in 1904, was the first cancer hospital in the nation, and the first to use radium to treat cancer patients. Fox Chase has been responsible for many firsts in cancer research.

Until 1927, cancer research had concentrated on studies of tumor tissues. That year, the Fox Chase Institute for Cancer Research, founded by Dr. Stanley P. Reimann, changed the course of cancer research by introducing the revolutionary approach of studying the basic mechanisms of normal cells.

Nobel Prize Awarded

The first identification of the hepatitis B virus was made at Fox Chase in 1967 and earned Dr. Baruch S. Blumberg, working with Dr. Irving Millman and other colleagues, the Nobel Prize in medicine in 1976. After the discovery, Blumberg's laboratory helped develop the hepatitis B vaccine, the first vaccine capable of preventing a human primary liver cancer.

PHARMACY

The Philadelphia College of Pharmacy and Science was the first such institution in the nation. Founded in Carpenters' Hall in 1821 as the College of Apothecaries, in 1921 it received the right to confer the degree of Bachelor of Science.

Dr. Baruch Blumberg (left) and Dr. Irving Millman confer at Fox Chase Cancer Center. Dr. Blumberg was awarded the Nobel Prize in medicine for the isolation of the hepatitis B virus. *Courtesy of Fox Chase Cancer Center*

SWALLOWING MADE EASIER

The earliest forms of medication were liquids and powders mixed in water or other liquids. It was Jacob Dunton, a Philadelphia wholesale druggist, who made the first compressed pills, or tablets, as early as 1862. His products were initially sold to pharmacists, then marketed under his own name in 1876. The definition of a tablet is a "compressed medicinal," and a pill is rolled from a "dough," not compressed. Pills really don't exist anymore, and capsules have replaced powders, so today we actually don't take pills, but capsules and tablets.

Elizabeth Marshall, the daughter of the president of the Philadelphia College of Pharmacy, became the first woman pharmacist when she took over the business owned by her father, Charles Marshall, and made it financially viable. She learned her profession through apprenticeship rather than formal training. She managed her father's pharmacy from 1804 until 1825, when it was sold to Charles Ellis and Izak Morris.

Too Strenuous

Women were considered physically unfit to be pharmacists because the substances used needed to be pounded with great force by hand, using an iron mortar and pestle. To ensure that the mortar would remain in place during such pounding, it had to be set on tree trunks that were driven into the floor, down to the basement!

However, a woman, Susan Hayhurst, was finally admitted to the College of Pharmacy and graduated in 1883 as both a pharmacist and a physician. She received her medical degree from Women's Medical College. Her double degrees were impressive enough to give her a position as head of the pharmacy department at Women's Medical College, where she remained for more than 30 years.

HERBAL MEDICINE TAKES ROOT

The first botanical garden for the cultivation of plants with medicinal properties was established in 1729 at Bachelor's Hall in the lower Wissahickon. This was actually the headquarters of a social club whose members were interested in science; in addition to promoting fellowship, the club raised and studied herbs for medicinal uses by cultivating a botanical garden attached to the building. Poet George Webb speaks of this place of retreat in a poem which he called "Bachelor's Hall":

...Then called with judgment each shall yield its juice,
Saliferous balsam to the sick man's use;
A longer date of life mankind shall boast,
And death shall mourn her ancient empire lost.

DRUG COMPANIES FLOURISH

Pharmaceutical manufacturers do more than sell drugs and allied products; they also research and create them. One of the most prolific of these companies, SmithKline Beecham, traces its origins to 1830, when John Smith opened a drugstore in Philadelphia. By 1875 his chief salesman, Mahlon Kline, had become a partner, and the company was renamed Smith Kline & Company. Smith Kline & Company brought out a number of products under its name, including Thorazine, the time-release capsule for depression that revolutionized the treatment of mental illness, and the ulcer medication Tagamet.

Several mergers and acquisitions took place over the years, and in 1989, SmithKline Beckman merged with the Beecham Group to form SmithKline Beecham. Beecham scientists had discovered the penicillin nucleus, 6-APA, in 1959. From this grew the manufacture of Amoxil, the most widely used antibiotic in the world, and Augmentin, today's gold standard in broad-spectrum antibiotics.

MORE FIRSTS

☆ The Humane Society of Philadelphia, organized in 1780, was the premier **first aid emergency organization**. Its object was the "recovery of drowned persons, and of those whose animation may be suspended from other causes, as breathing air contaminated by burning charcoal, hanging, exposure to the choke-damp of wells, drinking cold water while warm in summer, strokes of the sun, lightning, swallowing laudanum, etc."

☆ Not only the city of firsts but also the **city of first foundings**: The American Psychiatric Association was founded in Philadelphia in 1844, the American Medical Association in 1847, and the American Pharmaceutical Association in 1852. The American Medical Society was founded in 1773 by students who came from different American colonies to attend medical lectures.

☆ The **first school to award a diploma to nurses** was the School of Nursing of the Woman's Hospital of Philadelphia, in 1865. Harriet N. Phillips received the first diploma.

☆ When Dr. Arthur Goodspeed, who did pioneering work in x-ray development at the University of Pennsylvania in the 1890s, prepared to take the **first x-ray** photograph, he didn't do it on humans. Instead, he x-rayed coins in a coin purse.

☆ The **first school of chiropody** (now more commonly known as podiatry) was incorporated as a regular division of Temple University in 1915. Housed in an annex to Temple Hospital, the course graduated four students in its first class, after a 34-week program. Now, it's an extensive four-year course. Podiatry is the study and treatment of diseases of the feet. Practitioners are not M.D.'s, but Doctors of Podiatric Medicine.

☆ Rehabilitation centers got their start with Dr. Frank K. Krusen, who established the country's **first Department of Rehabilitative and Physical Medicine** at Temple University Hospital in 1929. This specialty of medicine involves rehabilitation programs for orthopedic problems, injuries, and post-surgical orthopedic repair. Occupational and physical therapists and speech pathologists are some of the people whose training is part of rehabilitative medicine. Today, some of these departments are called sports medicine.

☆ In 1935, Penn became the **first Ivy League school to offer a comprehensive degree program** (from bachelor's degree to doctorate) **in nursing**.

☆ The **first quadruplets delivered by cesarean section** were born on November 1, 1944, to Mr. and Mrs. Joseph Cirminello, in a Philadelphia hospital.

☆ The year 1952 was a big one for folks with cataracts, for it was then that Dr. Warren Snyder Reese fitted the first plastic lens at Wills Eye Hospital, the **first eye hospital in the country**, which was established here in 1832. Wills Eye played an important role in establishing ophthalmology as a separate medical specialty.

☆ Dr. Isadore S. Ravdin performed the **first televised surgical operation** on March 16, 1952, in the operating suite of the Hospital of the University of Pennsylvania.

☆ St. Christopher's Hospital for Children established the nation's **first tracheotomy unit for infants and children** in 1971 and, in 1989, became the first hospital in the world to use oxygen-rich liquid to help premature newborns breathe.

Food, Glorious Food

ICE CREAM, ANYBODY?

Ice cream, in all its delicious forms, had its creamy beginnings in our country in the City of Brotherly Love. Peter Bosse (sometimes spelled Bossu) was the owner of a candy store on South Fifth Street. He settled here from France in 1794 and is generally considered the creator of ice cream, introducing the concoction in 1801. However, Joseph Carre, of Eighth and Market Streets, was designated "ice cream seller" in a city directory dated 1795. He must have made it by hand, because the ice cream freezer wasn't invented until more than 50 years later. On October 3, 1848, Eber C. Seaman received a patent for the modern ice cream freezer, making commercial production and year-round ice cream sales possible.

DOLLEY MADISON SERVES ICE CREAM

The history books tell us that Dolley Madison was serving ice cream to her suitor, the future president, in 1787. Perhaps it was delivered by Joseph Carre down the street! Dolley didn't forget what a hit this creation made at her party. She served it as dessert at the second inaugural ball, held at the White House.

Bassett's Stays Around

Ice cream has always had many fans in Philly, and no brand more than Philadelphia's own Bassett's ice cream, which is the oldest ice cream producer in the country. Bassett's has been dishing out those delicious scoops since 1861. The business is still operated by direct descendants of the first Bassett ice cream maker.

Louis Dubois Bassett, a schoolteacher who knew a good thing, was an early moonlighter. In 1861, he opened a stand at Fifth and Market Streets to sell the first Bassett's ice cream. When Reading Terminal Market started selling food in 1893, Bassett's was there in all its creamy glory.

The Ice Cream Man

Ice cream hawkers cruising the streets, selling containers of ice cream, were the precursors to today's ice cream trucks that delight kids everywhere (at least those who are lucky enough to still have them in their neighborhoods). They were called "hokey pokey men," a phrase that originated in England. Today, "hokey pokey" is a popular ice cream flavor in New Zealand.

While Philadelphia can claim the introduction of ice cream as an American confection, ice cream actually goes back at least to medieval times, when drinks were cooled with ice and snow. And later, King Charles I of England offered a cook a job for life if he made him ice cream but kept the recipe a secret. The ice cream cone was a St. Louis invention; it made its debut in 1904.

THE FIRST CARBONATED BEVERAGES

Soda water came to us through a physician's curiosity. Early in the 19th century, famous Philadelphia surgeon Dr. Philip Syng Physick wanted to duplicate waters found in mineral springs, which people then (and now) considered to have beneficial health qualities. He asked for help from a local druggist, John Hart, who visited various springs and decided that adding a supersaturated solution of carbonic acid gas to water would achieve the doctor's wish. But the taste was medicinal. Another Philadelphia pharmacist, Townsend Speakman, added fruit juices in 1807 to improve the taste. Voilà! The soft drink. The concoction was used medicinally and dispensed to patients from fountains. Believers in its health benefits subscribed for $1.50 a month, which entitled them to one glass a day, every day.

A Flavor Breakthrough

Charles Elmer Hires, another entrepreneurial druggist, served the first root beer in 1875. Inspired by a concoction offered by his landlady, he combined roots and other items, such as the bark of sarsaparilla, sassafras, wild cherry, wintergreen, and ginger, and a very small amount of alcohol. Today's root beer is, of course, completely non-alcoholic.

Hires opened a drugstore in Philadelphia and placed a sign over his fountain that read "Hires Root Beer 5 cents." He exhibited his drink at the Centennial Exhibition, and it was an instant hit. He knew a good business when he saw it, so he founded the Charles E. Hires Company. At first he sold just the ingredients, along with instructions on how to blend them, but he started bottling and distributing his product sometime around 1893. Just a few years later he was selling it nationally, or at least through as much of a distribution system as existed nationally at that time.

Root beer is considered the original American soft drink. Today, Hires Root Beer is part of a vast soft drink and natural water industry owned by Dr Pepper/Seven-Up, Inc.

AN EXCEPTIONAL CONCOCTION

Put soda and ice cream together and what do you get? Ice cream soda, of course, which was first served here at the U.S. 50th Anniversary Exposition of the Franklin Institute. Concessionaire Robert M. Green sold a mix of carbonated water, cream, and syrup, but when he ran out of cream he substituted ice cream, hoping his customers wouldn't notice. They did—and they loved it! His sales jumped from $6 to $600 a day! He turned his creation into a real money maker and went on to found a company that manufactured soda fountains.

SCOUTING AND COOKIES

Girl Scouts and cookies go together, and they first paired up in Philadelphia in 1932. The Girl Scout organization was in financial straits, so it began fund-raising efforts. One of its early fund-raising projects was demonstrating the scouts' baking skills in the window of the Philadelphia Gas and Electric Company. The Girl Scouts sold their products right there, and the response was so good that they initiated Girl Scout Cookie Week in December 1934.

Cookie Competition

Initially, a box cost 23 cents; six boxes were $1.35. The program became a competitive effort among the troops, and by 1935, the regional council had raised enough money to pay its debts.

The success of the program soon motivated the national office to follow suit, and now the annual cookie program is the major fund-raiser for Girl Scout organizations throughout the nation. In 1997, 1,380 individual troops in southeastern Pennsylvania sold more than 1.6 million boxes of cookies and earned $754,000.

Girl Scouts Cook for Poor

Then and now, Girl Scouts of south-eastern Pennsylvania have used their cookie program as a fund-raiser. *Courtesy of the Girl Scouts of Southeastern Pennsylvania*

SWEETS AND SWEETER

To make ice cream, soft drinks, and cookies, you've got to have sugar. And in 1783, the first sugar refinery in the United States was founded in this city on Vine Street, right above Third. Dark brown raw sugar was imported from Cuba, Puerto Rico, the Philippines, and Hawaii, then processed and shipped to consumers all over the world. The rest is taste bud history.

Philadelphia remained a prolific sugar producer for many years. The Franklin Sugar Refinery grew to be the largest in the world, and by 1870, the combined refineries in Philadelphia produced almost $26,000 worth of the stuff—a good deal of money in those days.

In 1685, William Penn gave beer his stamp of approval, calling it "well boyled" and "a very tolerable drink" when infused with sassafras or pine. A few years later, the colonists started to experiment with ale.

Although Quakers frowned on the manufacture and consumption of spirits, they did not have the same opinion about beer. Several Friends operated quite profitable breweries in the mid-1600s. Anthony Morris' brewery, opened on Front Street below Walnut in 1687, was the oldest brewery continuing into the 20th century.

Brewers Parade Their Skills

As part of the mammoth celebration of independence that took place on July 4, 1788, a delegation of brewers marched in the parade with, as a local newspaper reported at the time, "ears of barley in their hats, and saches of hop vines, carrying malt shovels and mashing oars [and] a standard . . . decorated with the brewer's arms and the motto. . . 'Home brew'd is best.'"

HEATING COLD TURKEY

In 1750, two days before Christmas, Benjamin Franklin mistakenly attached the apparatus he used for his lightning experiments to himself instead of to his intended victim, a turkey. The jolt knocked him to the floor. We don't know how many turkeys Franklin electrocuted and cooked in his experiments, but he did declare that, when prepared by this method, they were "uncommonly tender." He wrote in his notebook that it took a lot more voltage to kill a turkey than a chicken!

MUSTARD

Philadelphians love mustard on their big Philly soft pretzels, as they have for decades. That's probably because it was first manufactured in this country in our city by Benjamin Jackson, who sold his product in glass bottles carrying his label. He advertised in 1768 that he was "the original establisher of the mustard manufactory in America . . . I brought the art with me into the country."

LET THEM EAT CAKE—AND THEY DID!

Bauer Brothers Bakery started in Pittsburgh in 1885 and sold its assets in 1913, but brother Philip wasn't finished with the baking business. He and his friend Herbert Morris came to Philadelphia in 1913 with a new idea: a cake that could be packaged at the place of manufacture and then distributed to stores everywhere. Previously, grocers had bought baked goods whole, then cut them into pieces, wrapped the pieces in paper, and sold them to customers.

A treat that Philadelphians away from home relish: Tastykakes. Shown are Krimpets, in all their delicious varieties. *Courtesy of Tasty Baking Company*

When the Philadelphia company started operations, it made its cakes, pan liners, and boxes by hand and sold them for 10 cents apiece. On the first day of sales, the cakes brought in big revenues—$28! Bauer and Morris were delighted and started the Tasty Baking Company. They experimented with recipes, especially for the icing, which was giving them trouble in Philadelphia's relatively humid weather. When it was perfected, they named their product "Tastykake." Now, from chocolate-covered cupcakes to creamy lemon pie, Tastykakes are a Philadelphia institution.

MAKING LIFE EASIER

To market their product, Philip Bauer and Herbert Morris created the Tastykake girl and put her on the package, along with the slogan "The Cake That Made Mother Stop Baking."

THE BOOK MEETS THE COOK

Started in 1985 to promote Philadelphia's restaurant renaissance, the Book and the Cook is the largest, most expansive annual food festival in the United States. Cookbook authors from all over the country come to present their recipes and demonstrate their creative talents. The event has grown over the years to include booths selling cookware items and specialty foods, food demonstrations, taste testings, and special dinners supervised by cookbook authors at local restaurants. Recently, it has added a cultural component: there are performances by the Philadelphia Ballet and the Philadelphia Orchestra, movies about food, exhibits of table decor by local designers, and even a traveling covered-dish supper.

One of the highlights of the fair is the annual presentation of the Toque Award at a special black tie event, to honor a top cookbook author of international repute. The 1998 recipient was Madeleine Kamman, author of *The New Making of a Cook: The Art, Techniques, and Science of Good Cooking* and *In Madeleine's Kitchen,* among other titles. Previous winners include Julia Child, Giuliano Bugialli, Craig Claiborne, Jacques Pepin, and Pierre Franey.

The 1998 Book and Cook event featured approximately 85 authors and 68 participating restaurants. Forty-five thousand visitors attended 92 dining events.

☞ **To Visit: The Book and the Cook**

The Book and the Cook is held each year in March at the Pennsylvania Convention Center. For information and tickets, contact:

The Book and the Cook
Center City Proprietors Foundation
1528 Walnut Street
Philadelphia, PA 19102
215-545-5353

ANOTHER KIND OF DINING

Fast food wasn't even a gleam in Ronald McDonald's eye when the ultimate in instant food retrieval started in Philadelphia on June 9, 1902. The automat introduced an entirely new concept in dining: self-service restaurants where food waited behind small glass doors. Many items cost five cents: people put a nickel in the slot, the door opened, and there was lunch. This automatic vending came at a time when people were fascinated with the novelty of "automation" and concerned about food cleanliness. The food in those dispensers seemed never to have been touched by human hands.

LINGER AT THE HEEL

Not only a place to eat, but also a place to talk, the Horn & Hardart restaurant on Broad Street near Locust was called "The Heel" by regulars, and it became a gathering place for local intellectuals, artists, writers, and table-hopping philosophers. Students and would-be playwrights, novelists, and pundits lingered over coffee, tea, and five-cent cakes for hours. In tough times, the ketchup on the table, poured into cups of free hot water, became a free meal, no questions asked.

The first H & H (Philadelphia's nickname for Horn & Hardart) restaurant opened at 818 Chestnut Street. Eventually, the chain expanded into retail outlets, day-old shops (freshness was such an important feature of the chain that it sold its leftover day-old products at a discount in separate stores), and even a few elite establishments with waitress service.

By the 1940s, H & H automats were feeding 10 percent of the city's population every day, with dishes like creamy macaroni and cheese, four different kinds of potatoes, chicken pies with thick brown gravy, creamed spinach, Harvard beets, and baked beans ("Less work for mother dear" was H & H's motto).

How H & H Got Started

On December 11, 1888, Joseph V. Horn opened a small lunchroom at 39 South 13th Street. His first day's gross was $7.25. He advertised for a partner, and Frank Hardart responded with "I'm your man."

By 1898, the partners had opened more eating establishments in downtown Philadelphia. Then Hardart had a new idea: he had seen automated equipment, a model for today's vending machines, in Germany, and

Those small glass doors don't open anymore, but they rekindle fond memories for Philadelphians who ate at Horn & Hardart.

thought it could be successful in Philadelphia. The first equipment Horn and Hardart ordered was sent over on a ship that sank on its way from Germany. But they were not deterred; they ordered more. Eventually, the partners improved upon the original German equipment and patented their changes. Then they promoted the idea that the automat assured the safe temperature of perishable foods, eliminating the possibility of food contamination.

In 1912, the Philadelphia-based company expanded into New York City and opened its first automat there, at 47th and Broadway. In its heyday, H & H had 147 restaurants, cafeterias, automats, and retail establishments in Philadelphia and New York. But alas, they were not to last. One by one, the automats closed down. The original Chestnut Street restaurant closed in December 1968, after 66 years of continuous operation. That gooey spaghetti and rich chocolate pudding no longer appeared like magic behind the glass doors.

PART OF AMERICANA

In May 1969, the equipment from the first automat was auctioned off. All but the brass knobs that released the 15-cent sandwiches and the distinctive gargoyle beverage spouts, that is. They found a home in the National Museum of American History at the Smithsonian Institution in Washington, D.C., where they can be seen today.

MORE FIRSTS

☆ With today's elegant houses and sophisticated restaurants of Society Hill, it's hard to imagine Dock Street as the **first center of food distribution** in the country. But in 1683, the earliest market shed was built near the waterfront to have access to the ferries that arrived daily with farm products.

☆ Elie Magloire Durand started the trend in fancy mineral waters in this country. In 1825, he **first bottled mineral water** and invented a machine for bottling it under pressure in a drugstore he ran at Sixth and Chestnut Streets.

☆ **Licorice** was invented in Philadelphia in 1900, and was followed by **bubble gum** in 1928.

☆ In 1986, Philadelphian Ian Cooper, who ran a dental supply business, invented the **pretzel cone** by combining two Philadelphia favorites: ice cream and pretzels.

Let Me Entertain You

C
H
A
P
T
E
R

9

THE PHILADELPHIA ZOO

For many firsts within a first, look to the Philadelphia Zoo. Forty-three species of American mammals, as well as Australian and Asiatic creatures including 10 marsupials, greeted visitors when the first American zoo opened its doors on July 1, 1874. Attendees then rode around in a goat cart; today's zoo visitors can use a monorail if they'd rather not walk.

Since its beginnings, the zoo has exhibited more than 500 species of animals. Along with the Portland, Oregon, zoo, the Philadelphia Zoo was the first to be accredited by the American Association of Zoological Parks and Aquariums in 1974.

LONG LIVE THE ANIMALS

Longevity records have been established for many animals at the Philadelphia Zoo, including several of the world's oldest recorded non-human primates. Massa, a lowland gorilla, lived to be 55 years old.

Famous Residents

The gorilla Massa was brought to the Philadelphia Zoo by animal rights advocate Gertrude Lintz when he was four years old. Years later he

The North Gate Entrance to the first zoo in the nation, the famous Philadelphia Zoo. Exhibits of rare and exotic animals have increased the zoo's popularity in recent years. *Courtesy of the Zoological Society of Philadelphia*

appeared in the movie *The Greatest Show on Earth*, trained by Martha Hunter, who later became a science teacher at Blue Bell's Oak Lane Day School. Hunter and Massa became great friends, and when she visited him at the zoo, it was clear to onlookers that good old pals were reuniting. A film about Massa's early years, *Buddy*, was made in 1997.

The famous naturalist Frank Buck brought Peggy, an Indian rhinoceros, and Bolivar, a six-ton elephant, from Ceylon. Bolivar was presented to the zoo as a Christmas present after touring with a circus. Perhaps the gesture was not totally generous; the elephant had already killed two handlers! The Philadelphia Zoo tamed him, and Bolivar lived for another 20 years.

Help for Animal Ailments

The zoo does more than showcase animals in enclosures that mimic nature; it's also internationally known for research in animal diseases and behavior, and for preservation of endangered species. From examinations of captive zoo animals that died from natural causes, medical researchers learned that certain animals could develop human diseases. And it was at this zoo that a skin test to detect tuberculosis in humans was developed. It came about during work to eradicate TB in zoo monkeys.

☞ To Visit: The Philadelphia Zoo

The Philadelphia Zoo
3400 West Girard Avenue
Philadelphia, PA 19104
215-243-1100
Hours: April-October: Monday-Friday, 9:30 A.M.-4:45 P.M., Saturday-Sunday, 9:30 A.M.-5:45 P.M.; November and March: daily, 9:30 A.M.-4:45 P.M.; December, January, and February: daily, 10 A.M.-4 P.M.
Closed Thanksgiving, Christmas, and New Year's Day.
Admission charged, except on Sunday mornings in December, January, and February, 10 A.M.-1 P.M., when admission is free.

THE SHOW MUST BEGIN

In 1724, the *American Weekly Mercury* reported a theatrical performance of "Roap Dancing" at the "New Booth on Society Hill." The previous year, the Pennsylvania Archives, which officially published records of events in Pennsylvania, had mentioned "comedians in town." Also in 1723, Philadelphia mayor James Logan was distressed that a company of itinerant players had "set up stage just without the verge of the town." And a puppet show, *Punch and Joan*, was presented in 1743 on Chestnut Street at the "Sign of the Coach and Horses." Despite these and, no doubt, other performances, the Quakers considered theater a form of entertainment that catered to people's baser instincts, and they ultimately barred theatrical productions in the city proper. But where there's a will . . .

William Plumsted's warehouse, situated as it was just over the city limits in Southwark, made it possible for theatrical companies to perform. The first recorded performance in this warehouse, by a company of players performing Joseph Addison's *Cato*, didn't have a long run. The players were banished.

The city fathers must have scared away potential producers and actors, as it took five years before another stage venture was attempted. In 1754, Lewis Hallam staged Nicholas Rowe's *The Fair Penitent* at Plumsted's warehouse. A few people in the audience came to the theater purely to voice their objections to the performance, but they were ejected before it even began. Hallam also staged *Tunbridge Walks, or The Yeoman of Kent*, and added a ballad opera, *The Country Wake, or Hob in the Well*.

The First Theater

Hallam's was a theatrical family, and when he died in 1756, his widow married David Douglass, a theater manager. They tried Philadelphia again. Douglass built a new theater in 1759, called the Theatre on Society Hill, but the season was brief and the theater closed. After more brouhahas about the unsuitability of theater, state and city powers supported the building of the Southwark Theatre in 1766. This became a permanent home for theatrical productions—the first in the nation. Religious groups petitioned city officials to prohibit the building, to no avail. This larger theater, built on the corner of South and Apollo Streets, was where the American Company performed. The first production of an American play was staged at the Southwark on April 24, 1767; it was *The Prince of Parthia*, written by Thomas Godfrey, Jr.

THE FOOTLIGHTS ARE ON

At some point, the city elders conceded that theater was here to stay, and the Chestnut Street Theatre, on the north side of Chestnut west of Sixth Street, was built in 1791. However, its opening was delayed until February

BRITISH GET IN THE ACT

The Southwark Theatre was closed in 1774 because of political unrest. It was reopened in 1777 by British officers during the occupation of Philadelphia, and they mounted amateur productions there.

17, 1794, because of the yellow fever epidemic. This was the city's first theater big enough to present plays and operas. It was considered the most elaborate theater in the country, featuring three galleries and French-style lighting, with oil lamps whose brightness could be adjusted depending on the mood on the stage.

In 1820 the original Chestnut Street Theatre was destroyed by fire, but it was rebuilt and became known in theatrical circles as Old Drury. The first opera by an American, *Leonora* by William H. Fry, was performed at the Chestnut Street Theatre in 1845. But when Jenny Lind was scheduled to perform in Philadelphia in 1850, under the sponsorship of P. T. Barnum (who auctioned off tickets for her performance), there was no auditorium in the city sufficient to accommodate all those who wanted to hear her, and no facility with proper acoustics. The city knew then that it needed another facility, the start of plans for the Academy of Music.

MORE FRIVOLITY, MORE FIRSTS

Not the first, but the oldest—and the home of many theatrical firsts—the Walnut Street Theatre officially opened at Ninth and Walnut Streets on February 2, 1809. A group of impresarios had purchased the property to build an amphitheater. When the Walnut was built, Thomas Jefferson was completing his second term as president, there were only 17 states, and Abraham Lincoln had not yet been born. The first theatrical production at

The exterior of the Walnut Street Theatre as it looked in 1880. The building has undergone many changes since then. *Courtesy of the Walnut Street Theatre*

the Walnut was Richard Sheridan's *The Rivals*, presented on January 1, 1812. Prior to that date, only circus acts were performed there. It is now the oldest theater in the nation in continuous operation.

When the Walnut opened, featuring equestrian acts, it was called the New Circus. It later went through many name changes: In 1811, it was called the Olympic. In 1820, when it was converted to a legitimate theater, it became the Walnut, but the name didn't stick. In 1822, the interior was restored to that of a circus and the Olympic name was revived for a time. Just a few years later, it became a distinctive "skyscraper," with an 80-foot dome. In August 1827, after being refurbished, the building reopened as the Philadelphia Theatre. More alterations took place the next year under the direction of famed architect John Haviland, who designed the facade, and the theater emerged as the Walnut in 1828.

In 1837, the Walnut became the first theater to install gas footlights. And although primitive, an air conditioner, "Mr. Barry's Patent Cool Air Machine," was added on June 15, 1855, making the Walnut the first theater to cool its patrons. In 1892, electricity came to the theater, replacing gas light with chandeliers and footlights.

J. Edwin Booth, the brother of Lincoln's assassin, John Wilkes Booth, was a silent partner with his brother-in-law, John Sleeper Clarke, when they purchased the Walnut for $100,000 in 1865. They managed it during the period when American theater was at the apex of its popularity, and then the Clarke family sold it in 1920, when motion pictures began to compete with live theater.

FIRST CURTAIN CALL

Legend has it that the tradition of the curtain call (opening the curtain after the performance ends so that performers can take another bow) started at the Walnut with a post-play appearance by famed actor Edmund Kean.

TO BE OR NOT TO BE...

A stagehand at the Walnut for 50 years, John "Pop" Reed left instructions in his will that his skull be used for the skull of Yorick in productions of *Hamlet*. Believe it or not, his wish was granted; Reed's skull was used in the play for many years. The skull now resides at the Van Pelt Library of the University of Pennsylvania.

... THE RULERS OF THE QUEEN'S NAVY

"Let every heart be filled with joy, and sing the praise of old Savoy" is the official song of the Savoy Company, organized in 1901—the first and oldest nonprofessional Gilbert and Sullivan performance group in the country. W. S. Gilbert, hearing of its existence, wrote from Grimm's Dyke, Harrow Weald, England, on June 15, 1904:

> I am much obliged to you for your note, giving interesting details of the work of the Philadelphia "Savoy Company." It is gratifying to know that the joint works of Sir Arthur Sullivan and myself are of sufficient interest to justify the formation of an amateur company for the express purpose of interpreting them. With every wish for your continued prosperity, I am, Faithfully yours, W. S. Gilbert.

Members of the Savoy Company perform in *The Mikado,* one of the many Gilbert and Sullivan productions that have entranced audiences for almost a century. *Courtesy of the Savoy Company*

Savoy was founded by Alfred Reginald Allen, a physician/neurologist on the staff of the University of Pennsylvania, whose hobby was music. The group's first production was *The Mikado*, performed at the Merion Cricket Club; the 1999 production is *Pirates of Penzance*, which will be performed at Longwood Gardens in Kennett Square and at the Academy of Music. The company has always been manned by volunteers, and proceeds from performances are distributed among selected charities.

From the beginning, the producers and performers took no liberties with score or libretto, and that still holds. Savoy performs all Gilbert and Sullivan operas in the original tradition, using Gilbert's own prompt books and stage directions. The group produces all 13 of the original Gilbert and Sullivan operas, doing one per season.

FIRST ACTORS' HOME

We hear much about the Actors' Home, in northern New Jersey, for actors who are aged and down on their luck. What many people don't realize is that the first actors' home was in Philadelphia. It opened on October 2, 1876, and was called the Forrest Home.

A THEATER IN THE PARK

The first municipally owned, operated, and supported theater-in-the-round was Philadelphia's Playhouse in the Park, which opened on June 30, 1951, with *Goodbye My Fancy*, featuring Conrad Nagel and Sylvia Sidney. A vast tent in Fairmount Park housed 1,072 seats; all profits went into the city coffers.

THE 50 YARD LINE

Television got its start about 1940, and the first commercially televised football game was reportedly one broadcast that year between Penn and the University of Maryland. WPTZ, the Philadelphia pioneer in telecasting, also televised one of the first collegiate football games—played on September 26, 1941, between Temple University and the University of Kansas, at Temple Stadium. Temple won.

Temple Stadium witnessed another football first—the first professional football game in which 10 touchdowns were made. It happened on November 7, 1934, when the Philadelphia Eagles defeated the Cincinnati Reds, 64-0.

LEGAL KICKS

The first use of the placement kick from scrimmage was used by Penn in an 1897 game against Harvard.

Played by the Numbers

Penn's football team was the first to wear complete uniforms, in an 1876 game against Princeton. Numbers took a few more years, but by 1913, Penn's players' jerseys sported numbers in a game against the University of Wisconsin. They were the first uniforms to identify players in this way.

TAKE ME OUT TO THE BALL GAME

Until 1863, baseball was a game of amateurs. But when the Philadelphia Athletics hired Alfred J. Reach, second baseman of the Brooklyn Eckfords, for a salary of $25 a week, professional baseball started. And the first baseball player to hit four consecutive home runs in one game did so in Philadelphia in a game against the Athletics. Lou Gehrig of the New York Yankees scored home runs in the first, fourth, fifth, and seventh innings on June 3, 1932.

Long before that, on October 1, 1865, the Philadelphia Athletics defeated the Jersey City Nationals by scoring more than 100 runs in a nine-inning game.

THE GLOVED ONE

In the 1880s, Phillies shortstop Arthur Irwin became the first infielder to wear a glove. He designed and patented his glove and sold the patent to the Reach-Shibe firm.

The first National League game, played in Philadelphia on April 22, 1876, at 25th and Jefferson Streets, matched the Philadelphia Athletics against the Boston Red Stockings. Boston won, 6-5. Not long after, on May 1, 1883, the Philadelphia Phillies played their first game at Recreation Park, 24th Street and Columbia Avenue, against the Providence Grays. Twelve hundred spectators watched as the Grays defeated the Phillies, 4-3.

TO THE FINISH LINE

Relay races may be an integral part of the Olympics today, but that wasn't always so. The first recorded relay race occurred on May 12, 1892, between Penn and Princeton. Princeton won, but the tables turned to Penn's advantage the following year.

The race initiated Philadelphia's hosting of the annual Penn Relays, the oldest and largest competition of its kind. First held in 1895, this event introduced the use of a baton and metric measurements in relay races. Fourteen thousand competitors participated in the races in 1997.

LIGHTS, CAMERA, ACTION

Movies started before the turn of the century in Philadelphia. Keith's Bijou Theater, at Eighth and Race Streets, showed the first crude motion pictures on flexible film way back in 1896. The films had been exhibited at the Franklin Institute in 1894 by C. Franklin Jenkins. And movie producer Sigmund Lubin created his studio production in 1897, a year after he took the first moving picture of his horse eating hay.

Lubin's Theaters

Lubin was an optician who started to show films on the roof of the Dime Museum in 1898. The Dime Museum—which had many names, including the American Museum—was not really a museum, but a theater. It featured vaudeville, plays, minstrel shows, and other forms of entertainment. Later, Lubin built a motion picture theater, called Lubin's Cineograph, at the National Export Exposition on the banks of the Schuylkill. In 1899, he opened the country's first real motion picture theater at Seventh and Market Streets.

Then Lubin got involved not just in showing movies but also in making them. His first—and quite primitive—movie studio was at 916 Arch Street. By 1915, his studio was one of the largest in the country. He had a large facility at 20th Street and Indiana Avenue and one of the largest outdoor studios in the country near Valley Forge.

The First Docudrama

In 1897, a boxing match between Jim Corbett and Bob Fitzsimmons was filmed by the Veriscope Company, which owned the release rights. It announced that the film would be released two months later. Not to be outdone, Lubin hired some actors to recreate the fight on the roof of his Arch Street film studio, using a newspaper account of the fight as the script. He shot the phony fight and advertised its release a month before the legitimate film was shown—and managed to get a copyright on his sham!

First Flickerings

Lubin was preceded in an elementary fashion by Dr. Coleman Sellers and Henry Renno Heyl. There were hints of Disney when, in 1860, Sellers made the first photographs of motion and, the following year, patented the equipment to exhibit them. Heyl invented the Phasmatrope, a converted projecting lantern with a revolving disc containing 16 openings near the edge. He placed photographic plates on the edge to produce the first animated photographic picture projection, which was witnessed by a theater audience on February 5, 1870, at the Ninth Annual Entertainment of the Young Men's Society of St. Mark's Evangelical Lutheran Church, at the Academy of Music. Almost 20 years later, Thomas Edison used Sellers' and Heyl's principles in his own experiments.

TV EXPERIMENTS WITH PROGRAMMING

The first western television show was produced and broadcast by WCAU-TV from 1953 to 1954. It was called *Action in the Afternoon* and lasted two seasons. The live show featured "Old Buck," a fifteen-year-old cow pony from Air-Mount Stables.

The first pay television broadcast of a sporting event was the closed-circuit telecast of the Jersey Joe Walcott–Rocky Marciano fight at Municipal

Stadium on September 23, 1952. The fight was telecast coast to coast; Marciano won the heavyweight title by a knockout in the 13th round.

MOVIES AND TV JOIN

New York City and Schenectady, New York, joined Station WPTZ of Philadelphia in broadcasting the first television premiere of a motion picture on April 10, 1944. It was a two-reel short called *Patrolling the Ether*.

Possibly more entertainment than politics, the 1940 Republican national convention, held in Philadelphia, was the first telecast of a political convention. An NBC station covered the convention over a five-day period, with 33 hours of coverage.

Bandstand Goes National

Was it *Bandstand*, and his association with so many teenagers, that has kept Dick Clark perpetually young? *Bandstand*, the first and most popular teenage television show of the 1950s, had its start at the WFIL studios in the Arena at 46th and Market Streets.

In 1952, the station needed some visuals onscreen while music played in the background so that it could produce the television equivalent of radio music shows. High school teenagers were invited to dance. When the station incorporated the popular rock and roll sound into its traditional music, the show became a sensation, and so did its disc jockey and emcee, Dick Clark. For the first few years, the DJ/emcee had been Bob Horn, who had had teenagers jitterbugging to acceptable popular music, pointedly avoiding the more tempestuous rock and roll. But in 1956, when Clark replaced Horn, he included rock and roll and the show, now called not just *Bandstand* but *American Bandstand*, went national.

MUSIC, MUSIC, MUSIC

On January 7, 1820, a group of music supporters met at Elliott's Hotel at Sixth and Chestnut Streets to institute a society to provide funds for the relief and support of "decayed musicians and their families." The Musical Fund Society they founded fulfilled that purpose, along with its primary goal: to advance music, both sacred and secular, by presenting fine compositions to the public.

WE STILL LISTEN TO THE RADIO

"Uncle Wip" was a fixture on radio station WIP in the late 1930s and '40s. He was the emcee of the first children's talent show in the United States heard over the airwaves. Uncle Wip was really Wayne Cody, a relative of Buffalo Bill Cody's.

As early as 1924, Cody was a vaudeville performer under contract to RKO. He played all the vaudeville houses and was first heard on radio on Philadelphia's WCAU. His wife, Ethel May, ran a voice school for children, and her husband's popular Sunday-morning program became a showcase for top students. Cody was a popular figure among entertainers, garnering 600 fan letters a week and 1,000 greeting cards on his birthday.

MORE FIRSTS

☆ Musical Fund Hall, on Locust Street, is the **oldest music hall** in the United States, built in 1824.

☆ Mrs. John Drew, mother of actor John Drew 2nd and grandmother of the famous Barrymores, was the first **woman theater manager**. She managed the Arch Street Theatre for 30 years after her husband's death in 1850. It was at this theater that her son made his stage debut in *Cool as a Cucumber*.

☆ Shakespeare has been around for a long time, but he didn't make his way into "society" in the United States until the **first Shakespeare Society** was founded at the University of Pennsylvania in 1852.

☆ The **first accordion patent** was issued to Anthony Faas of Philadelphia on January 13, 1854.

☆ The **first indoor football game** was played, believe it or not, on the parquet floors of the Academy of Music on March 7, 1889.

☆ Long before the popularity of the slam dunk, **college basketball using five-man teams** was first tried in an 1897 Penn vs. Yale game. Before this new way of playing the game was initiated, each side used nine players at a time.

☆ **Baseball's American League** was first organized in Philadelphia on January 29, 1900, with eight teams. The franchises were located in Philadelphia, Washington, Baltimore, Boston, Chicago, Cleveland, Detroit, and Milwaukee.

☆ The **first black American to win an Olympic gold medal** for the 4 x 400-meter relay was University of Pennsylvania graduate John Baxter Taylor, Jr., in 1908.

☆ The **first golfer to play 180 holes in one day**, and the initiator of the marathon contest (a contest to see who can last the longest in a golf game), was Edward Styles. On July 11, 1919, at the Old York Road Country Club, he played from 5:53 A.M. until 8:32 P.M.

☆ Phillies pitcher Hugh Mulcahy became the **first major league player drafted by the U.S. Army in World War II**.

☆ Remember Chubby Checker and the **Twist**? Those gyrations started here, some say, inspired by the shape of the soft twisted pretzel.

Over Land, Sea, and Air

FIRST AUTOMOBILE

Officially called the Orukter Amphibolis (Latin for "amphibious dredge"), the first "automobile" was propelled by steam and could navigate on land or water. In 1805, Oliver Evans was commissioned by the Philadelphia Board of Health to manufacture a scow, which was a dock cleaning machine. He built a steam-operated, amphibious vehicle called an amphibious digger, which was mounted on wheels and operated by a five-horsepower engine. It was 30 feet long and 12 feet wide. When it was used as a scow, a chain of buckets scooped up mud. And when a carriage was mounted on it, it became a steam land carriage. Evans propelled it from his shop, around Centre Square, and to the Schuylkill River, lowering it on its wheels. Then, using a stern paddle-wheel, he sailed it up the river.

PAYING FOR THE SHOW

Oliver Evans placed an ad in the *Philadelphia Gazette*, asking citizens who viewed his Orukter Amphibolis to contribute 25 cents for the privilege, half to be used by him for further inventions, and half to go to his workmen, who contributed their time to construct it.

Evans also built the first steam engine in the United States. But people didn't believe him when, in 1804, he said he could "make a carriage go by steam on a level road faster than any horse." When he rolled this machine out of his workshop, it was the most remarkable transportation vehicle the world had seen to date, and one of the first horseless carriages.

EVANS' IRON WORKS

Oliver Evans' Mars Iron Works, at Ninth and Race Streets, was one of the nation's leading steam-engine manufacturers. Evans became a successful builder of high-pressure engines, including the high-powered steam engine that first ran the Fairmount Water Works.

BURN THAT RUBBER!

Oliver Evans' wheels were made of wood; rubber tires weren't available yet. It wasn't until 1839 that Charles Goodyear invented vulcanized rubber. Rubber existed before that, but it froze in cold weather and became gluey in heat. Goodyear worked with the raw product to perfect it. Before his success, he went bankrupt in the hardware business in Philadelphia and spent some time in debtor's prison. (His family was often impoverished to the point of hunger, and six of his children died of disease and starvation.) While in jail, Goodyear asked his wife to bring him some raw rubber and a rolling pin so he could do some experiments in his cell. He called his creation "elastic gum," and the product was named after Vulcan, the Roman god of fire.

Persistence Pays Off

Once Goodyear was out of prison, he and his wife and children made magnesia-dried rubber overshoes in their kitchen. But to their disappointment, during the summer, the substance melted into a sticky rubber mess. Complaints from the neighbors about the smelly substance forced Goodyear to move to New York, where he continued his experiments. When he finally achieved the right chemical mix that made rubber stay firm but pliable in any weather, he was jubilant and envisioned all sorts of things made of rubber—even bank notes and jewelry!

Neither Goodyear nor his family was ever connected with the company that bears his name. The only direct descendant is U.S. Rubber, which once absorbed a small company in which Goodyear served as director. He never benefited financially from the vast rubber empire that exists today, but he seemed not to care about money. He once wrote: "Life should not be estimated exclusively by the standard of dollars and cents. I am not disposed to complain that I have planted and others have gathered the fruits. A man has cause for regret only when he sows and no one reaps."

THE HIGHWAYS AND BYWAYS

The first macadam road was the Lancaster Turnpike, 62 miles long, connecting Philadelphia and Lancaster. Work was started in 1793 by the Philadelphia and Lancaster Turnpike Railroad Company and completed in December 1795. By 1828, private and public projects were underway to create a network of turnpikes, bridges, and canals to connect Philadelphia to the rest of Pennsylvania and to surrounding states.

Around 1795, the trip to New York from Philadelphia took a very long day, from about 4 A.M. until after sunset, and required five stagecoach changes and two river crossings—across the Delaware and the Raritan on scows. Travelers made the trip on the first road north out of Philadelphia, which was built on top of a former Indian path between Philadelphia and Morrisville, New Jersey.

WE TAKE TO THE TRACKS

The first experimental railroad track was constructed for Thomas Leiper so that he could haul stone from the Delaware to Crum Creek. The cars, built by a Scotch millwright named Somerville, were hauled along the track by horses. The tracks were then laid down in a yard adjoining the Bulls' Head Tavern in Northern Liberties.

Those old-fashioned wooden railroad tracks, 180 feet in length, were tried out in July 1809 when a carriage with four grooved wheels was placed on the tracks and a horse, walking between them, pulled 10,696 pounds up the track. This was the first railroad prototype built in the United States. Leiper considered the experiment so successful that he went on to build the first railroad to transport stone from his quarries on Crum Creek to his landing in Delaware County, a distance of about one mile.

BRING ON THAT STEAM HEAT

Although small potatoes by today's standards of rocket travel, when Matthias Baldwin undertook the job of designing and building a steam engine capable of pulling two carriages, his achievement was greeted with cheers by onlookers. Baldwin didn't have transportation in mind at the time—only entertainment. Franklin Peale, manager of the Franklin Institute, encouraged Baldwin to build the huge steam engine because he thought it would be a major attraction for his patrons. It was supposed to be large enough to pull two carriages around a track laid on the museum floor. It's still there, and there is probably no Philadelphia school child who hasn't taken a ride on "Old Ironsides." When the managers of the Germantown and Morristown Railway Company saw it, they were so impressed that they asked Baldwin to build them a steam locomotive, which they considered a vast improvement over horse power.

Baldwin made this first engine with his own hands, creating his own tools and training workmen. Old Ironsides was tested on April 25, 1831, on

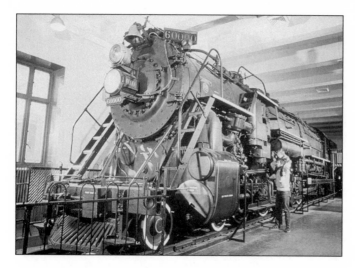

The first Baldwin locomotive, still on display and still giving children a sample train ride in the basement of the Franklin Institute. *Courtesy of the Franklin Institute Science Museum*

a railroad track laid down in the Philadelphia Museum Arcade on Chestnut Street, and it stayed there on exhibition for a while.

This granddaddy of American railroads made its debut on November 23, 1832. Old Ironsides flew over the tracks at a speed of 30 miles an hour, but wasn't permitted out in the rain. Instead, horses pulled the passenger cars in inclement weather. The engine later ran for several months on a railroad track at Smith's Labyrinth Garden on Arch Street.

TRAIN SIGNALS

The first railroad signal system of block signals (a method of fixed or wayside signals along the tracks that divide the railroad into sections, or blocks, spaced so that trains run at safe distances from each other) was installed between Philadelphia and Trenton in 1863 along what was called the Philadelphia and Trenton Railroad, now part of Amtrak. In the days before train signals, local trains just waited for faster, long-distance trains to pass before they proceeded on the tracks so that they could avoid any chance of collisions.

PROGRESS SOMETIMES CAUSES ACCIDENTS

On July 17, 1856, William S. Lee, the careless engineer of a local train (he was a dentist by profession, moonlighting as a train engineer), didn't wait for a faster train to pass, and there was a collision near Fort Washington, outside Philadelphia. Sixty-six lives were lost that day. The conductor of the other train, fearing he would be blamed, committed suicide. The accident inspired the first American song commemorating a train wreck, "The Killed by the Accident on the North Pennsylvania Railroad, July 17th, 1856." It was followed by another commemorative ballad, "Verses on the Death of Miss Annie Lilly."

Railroad travel was getting better all the time, and the first gasoline-mechanical cars were placed in regular service by the Pennsylvania Railroad in 1923. The cars ran on the Berwick, Flemington, and Bustleton lines in the Philadelphia district, but were replaced by gasoline-electric cars in 1926.

RIDING THE SEAS

The world's first regularly scheduled steamboat service was inaugurated on July 14, 1790. The site of this singular event was the Arch Street Ferry. John Fitch, an inventor, had demonstrated to President Washington that harnessed steam could power a boat. The first skiff steamboat had been operated on the Delaware River in 1786, and on August 22, 1787, Fitch's 45-foot steamboat had navigated the Delaware, watched by the members of the Constitutional Convention. Within a few years, a steamboat service operated between Philadelphia and Trenton.

Cruise Ship Forerunners

That summer of 1790, the first steamboat operated for passengers and freight ran on the Delaware, stopping at Philadelphia, Burlington, Bristol, Chester, Wilmington, and other stops along the way. Regularly scheduled trips were advertised, and 17,000 miles were logged over that summer— 17 years before Robert Fulton's steamboat took its first ride on the Hudson.

Water Traveling Becomes Popular

The boat traveled about three miles an hour (which is a good walking speed). A subsequent boat got up to eight miles an hour and ran between the Arch Street Ferry and Trenton. The first voyage between Lake Erie and Philadelphia was made under the stewardship of John Thompson and David Lummis on the schooner *Whitefish*. It took a complicated and circuitous route from Erie City via Buffalo. Part of the trip was made by land, where the boat was hauled by a wagon, eventually going along the Jersey coast to Cape May and then up the Delaware to Philadelphia. The *Whitefish*, recovering from this arduous journey, resided in Peale's Museum and then in the State House yard until it fell apart.

BOATS NEED INSURANCE

The Insurance Company of North America was formed in 1792, the first of its kind. Within six years of its formation, the company was writing virtually all the marine insurance in the country. It also issued a few life insurance policies—the first to Philadelphian John Holker in 1796.

PRIZES FOR FLYING

The *Philadelphia Ledger* and the *New York Times* cooperated in offering a $10,000 prize for the first airplane round trip between two large cities that was completed in one day. It was won by Charles Keeney Hamilton, who flew a Curtiss biplane from Governors Island, New York, to Philadelphia. He left New York at 7:36 A.M., arriving at Front Street and Erie Avenue at 9:26 A.M. With a short detour in New Jersey on the way back—he landed in a swamp in South Amboy to repair a broken spark plug—he returned to Governors Island. The stop delayed his return to New York until evening, but his actual round-trip flying time was 3 hours and 34 minutes.

MORE FIRSTS

☆ The **first public canal company**, the Schuylkill and Susquehanna Canal Company, was chartered in Philadelphia in 1791. Offered at $200 each, 1,000 shares were put up for sale. Businessman and banker Robert Morris was president of the company.

☆ Philadelphian Eleazer A. Gardner invented the **first cable car** in 1858. A series of pulleys inside an underground tunnel housed the cable.

☆ The **first electric streetcars** started in Philadelphia in 1892.

☆ We still experiment with and agitate over the advisability of **electric cars**, but they first came on the scene in 1894, patented on August 31 by two Philadelphians, Henry G. Morris and Pedro G. Salom.

☆ The automobile was here to stay, and inventions to improve it came quickly. Both the **first stamped auto bodies and auto body coating** were created in this city in 1912.

☆ The **first airmail delivery** took place on May 15, 1918, when the War Department sponsored an experimental airmail route between New York City, Philadelphia, and Washington. Two sacks of mail left Belmont Field on Long Island and flew to Philadelphia; some of the mail was deposited here, and the rest went on to Potomac Field in Washington, D.C.

☆ The **first amphibious seaplane** glider was made of wood and was 40 feet long, with a 72-foot wingspan. Twelve men and lots of equipment were aboard when the XL-Q-1 glider was launched in January 1943 from the Philadelphia Naval Shipyard. The glider was meant to be used as a troop transport and cargo carrier.

Buildings and Bridges

PRESERVING THE PAST

Despite the constant sound of bulldozers and concrete mixers, tearing down and building up, Philadelphia takes great pride in its old buildings and has an active historic preservation program. This is nothing new for the city; in 1749, Peter Kalm, an agricultural explorer from Uppsala, Sweden, wrote about how Philadelphia was saving old structures. He was referring specifically to Swanson House, a log house near Swanson and Beck Streets that belonged to Sven Swanson and was considered the city's oldest structure. At the time, English speculators were coming into the area and tearing down old structures to build new brick houses.

Original Architecture

The Athenaeum building, at 219 South Sixth Street, was the first Renaissance Revival building in the city. It was built in 1845 and is now the principal repository of architectural records in the city. The Athenaeum was founded in 1814 to collect materials "connected with the history and antiquities of America, and the useful arts, and generally to disseminate useful knowledge" for public benefit. At first called the Architectural Library of Philadelphia, its collection was then housed with the American Philosophical Society.

The first person to become a member of the Architectural Library was the famous Philadelphia architect William Strickland. In his writing, he predicted that railroads would supersede canals, which, of course, is what happened. Strickland was responsible for designing many public buildings, such as the Second Bank of the United States, a portion of Independence National Historical Park, and the Chestnut Street Theatre.

FIRST RECORD

The first antiquarian architectural record in the Architectural Library of Philadelphia's collection was William Strickland's drawing of Anthony Benezet's house on Chestnut Street. The drawing was commissioned by Robert Vaux before the house was demolished in March 1818.

Between 1836 and 1845, the Athenaeum sponsored a competition that invited leading American architects to submit designs for its new architectural library and reading room. John Notman won. Notman's building gave America its first urban structure in Italianate Revival, which went on to become a popular building style in the country at that time. The library maintains a collection of original drawings, including Strickland's submission for the competition, and Robert Mills' drawings of the Pennsylvania State House (which became Independence Hall).

☞ To Visit: The Athenaeum Public Gallery

The Athenaeum
East Washington Square, 219 South Sixth Street
Philadelphia, PA 19106
215-925-2688
Hours: Monday-Friday, 9 A.M.-5 P.M.
Appointments necessary for tours and research.
Admission free.

REACHING TO THE SKY

The PSFS building, built in 1932, is considered the country's first modern skyscraper. It was also the first to be completely air-conditioned. In 1969, the local chapter of the American Institute of Architects called it "the building of the century."

EARLIER SKYSCRAPERS?

We might call Christ Church and Independence Hall the first Philadelphia skyscrapers, as their towers broke the symmetry of the low skyline of two-story houses, then the norm.

When it was built, the Philadelphia Saving Fund Society building was the world's tallest skyscraper, and the first building of its size to be air-conditioned. Though no longer PSFS, it remains a monument to Philadelphia architecture. *Courtesy of Edward Savaria, Jr., for Mellon Bank, N.A.*

The conservative board of PSFS (Philadelphia Saving Fund Society) had to be persuaded to accept the revolutionary design of the first international-style skyscraper, designed by George Howe and William Lescaze. PSFS no longer exists and the building is being redeveloped for other purposes, but the city has been assured that the huge neon PSFS sign atop the building, a Philadelphia landmark, will remain.

OVER THE DELAWARE

Until 1926, the only way to get from Camden to Philadelphia was by ferry. There were talks way back in 1818 about spanning the Delaware River at Philadelphia; city fathers saw that the bridge at Trenton was a boon to business and wanted one, too. Finally, in 1914, when the Delaware River Bridge and Tunnel Commission was created, bridge construction in Philadelphia started. Twelve years and more than $37 million later, the 1.81-mile-long, 125½-foot-wide span was completed—the longest suspension bridge in the world, and known merely as the Delaware River Bridge. On opening day, July 1, 1926, no vehicle traffic was allowed so that thousands of pedestrians could stroll along the traffic lanes.

The city had a beautiful new bridge, but that didn't mean commuters had to use it; many continued taking the ferry to and from work. Why? Because the ferry was cheaper: it only cost a nickel, and the bridge toll was a whopping 25 cents!

DAREDEVILS

Three weeks after the bridge opened, a *Philadelphia Inquirer* airplane flew under it. The following month, a navy dirigible, the *Los Angeles*, flew over it.

On January 17, 1955, the bridge was renamed the Benjamin Franklin Bridge to commemorate Franklin's 250th birthday. And to celebrate the 200th anniversary of the drafting of the Constitution, the bridge was lit up like a birthday cake with hundreds of high-intensity lights.

CHURCH'S CLOSE CALL

St. George's United Methodist Church, built in 1769, is the oldest Methodist church in continuous use in the United States. With its gleaming white steeple, it was a stunning structure. But it had one major fault—it was in the way. The church was sitting right where the new bridge was to be. "It has to go," argued bridge builders. "No!" cried preservationists. And so the church was saved. The bridge was moved 14 feet south, Fourth Street was lowered, and a flight of steps was added to reach the ground floor of St. George's.

Historic St. George's United Methodist Church and the Historical Center at the foot of the Benjamin Franklin Bridge. Note the steps that were added when Fourth Street was lowered to make way for the bridge. *Courtesy of St. George's United Methodist Church*

More Bridges

The bridge at the Falls of Schuylkill was only two years old when it collapsed. It had been held up by chains (it was called the "chain bridge"), and the weight of crossing cattle was just too much. It was rebuilt, but some years later it collapsed again. This time, a narrow footbridge designed only for people, not for vehicles or cattle, was erected in its place by Philadelphia manufacturers Captain Josiah White and Erskine Hazard. This bridge, the first known wire suspension bridge, was opened to foot traffic in June 1816. White and Hazard were taking no chances this time—they limited traffic to a maximum of eight people at a time. And they charged for the privilege of crossing—one cent per person until the building cost ($125) was recovered.

The first successful wire bridge in America, considered an engineering masterpiece in its time, was constructed in Philadelphia in 1842 by Charles Ellet, who later built a suspension bridge across the Potomac River. His Philadelphia bridge connected Spring Garden Street with West Philadelphia. About 30 years later, it was replaced by a steel structure, called the Callowhill/Spring Garden Street Bridge; in 1964 this, too, was demolished and replaced with the present structure, now simply called the Spring Garden Street Bridge.

BRIDGES GET BIGGER

The Upper Ferry Bridge was built across the Schuylkill just below Fairmount Street to replace a floating bridge that had been washed away. It was a single wooden arch 340 feet long, which was 98 feet longer than the longest bridge in North America at the time. The crest of the arch rose 30 feet into the air, and the roadway started from a broad base and tapered to 20 feet in the center. Fire destroyed it in 1838.

The Girard Avenue Bridge was built for the Centennial Exhibition and was considered the widest bridge in the world (100 feet) when it was completed in 1874. Parts of its original iron railing are now exhibited in the Smithsonian Institution in Washington, D.C.

BOATHOUSES ALONG THE SCHUYLKILL

From the West River Drive, you can see lights twinkling at night on the clubhouses that fringe the Schuylkill along Boathouse Row. On Kelly Drive (formerly the East River Drive), these beautiful Victorian buildings appear just around the bend, housing Philadelphia's famous sculling clubs. They're the oldest architecture of their type in the nation.

Sculling on the Schuylkill is a Philadelphia tradition, first organized by the Barge Club of the University of Pennsylvania. By the 1850s, rowing clubs had begun building shelters to house their sculls and oars. As the clubs' use increased to include social functions, more substantial structures were built, each more fanciful than the next.

A different rowing club owns each house, and all except one are made of brick or stone. Once it was clear that the boathouses were to become permanent, well-known architects were hired to design them. The Undine Barge Club was designed by Frank Furness and David Evans, Jr., and built in 1883; the Malta Boat Club, designed by G. W. & W. D. Hewitt, was built in 1870. The University of Pennsylvania owns one boathouse, and the rest are privately owned, on land leased from the city's Department of Recreation.

A MINI WATER CROSSING

A lighthouse at the northern end of the boathouses once directed Schuylkill excursion steamers returning from evening cruises to the Wissahickon Creek or the Manayunk section of Philadelphia.

A Private Navy

The Schuylkill Navy oversees the activities of the boat clubs. Founded in 1858, it is the oldest amateur athletic governing organization in the United States. The job of the Navy is to "secure united action among the several clubs and to promote amateurism on the Schuylkill River." The group also organizes the annual Schuylkill Navy Cross-Country Run (or Turkey Trot) each Thanksgiving Day, and in 1999 it will host the U.S. Rowing Annual.

Olympic Champions

Boathouse Row has produced many Olympic sculling champions. In 1920, John B. Kelly—Philadelphia brick company owner and millionaire, once a candidate for mayor, and father of Princess Grace of Monaco—won two Olympic sculling titles on the same day, earning gold medals in both single and double sculling events. In 1924, he and Paul Costello won again in the double sculls. Winning in two consecutive Olympics was a first for American sculling teams.

At the 1956 Games, John Kelly, Jr. and Paul Costello, Jr., sons of the 1924 winners, won medals in rowing. At almost every Olympic rowing competition since the late 19th century, U.S. teams have included at least one representative from Boathouse Row. For more than a century, Philadelphia has been a major training point for the country's rowing sport.

SCULLING PRESERVED

One of Thomas Eakins' famous paintings, *Max Schmitt in a Single Scull*, shows Eakins' high-school friend resting on his oars as he rows on the Schuylkill. The painting is part of the collection of the Metropolitan Museum of Art in New York City.

Women Rowers

The building at Number 14 Boathouse Row, which now houses the Philadelphia Girls' Rowing Club, was built in 1861 to house the Philadelphia Skating and Humane Society. This club had started to petition the city in 1855 to build a site on the banks of the river. At first, the building housed a hospital and "apparatus used for rescuing persons from a watery grave." The Philadelphia Skating Club sold its Boathouse Row headquarters to the Philadelphia Girls' Rowing Club in 1938.

THE CITY OF HOMES

Elfreth's Alley, the oldest street in the United States in continuous use, was named after a blacksmith who came to Philadelphia in 1690 and whose family later owned all the properties on the street. It was created in 1703, when two property owners decided they wanted to divide their land with a passageway for carts. Most of the houses on the alley were rented by craftsmen. Typical was Number 126, occupied by a dressmaker whose shop was on the first floor, with living quarters above. This house is now the Elfreth's Alley Museum. By the end of the 18th century, the alley looked much as it looks today: a narrow cobblestone street lined with charming, small row homes.

☞ *To Visit: Elfreth's Alley Association, Home of Elfreth's Alley Museum*

Elfreth's Alley Association
126 Elfreth's Alley
Philadelphia, PA 19106
215-574-0560
Hours: Tuesday-Saturday, 10 A.M.-4 P.M.; Sunday, 12-4 P.M.
Closed weekdays in January and February.
Tours continuous when museum is open.
Admission free.

Elfreth's Alley, the oldest street in the United States still in use, continues to attract tourists to its picturesque homes. *Courtesy of the Elfreth's Alley Association*

FROM TRAIN SHED TO CONVENTION CENTER

When Reading Terminal was completed, its arched shed was the largest single-span structure in the world. It is still the largest such building in the country today.

The introduction of steam locomotives eliminated the fear of fire from wood-burning engines, which meant that the Reading Railroad Company could build an inner-city terminal. When the terminal was built in 1891, it was actually two buildings: Head House, which contained waiting rooms and administrative offices, and the shed, which covered the train platforms.

Before the site was a train terminal, it was the home of the Franklin Farmer's Market, which had sold food there since 1860. Now, once again, a food market—the Reading Terminal Market—is located there. The famous shed has been incorporated into the new Pennsylvania Convention Center, whose ballroom, meeting rooms, and grand hall are all under the dramatic skylight in the shed roof.

A PLANNED CITY

Philadelphia was the first planned city in the new country. In 1682, William Penn's surveyor, Thomas Holme, came from England to lay out the plans, purchasing land for Penn between the Delaware and Schuylkill Rivers. Holme's plan established a grid, with streets broken by public squares, each eight acres with a central square for civic buildings. These public squares were the first planned parks in the nation.

The city was an economic enterprise for Penn; he sold lots to prospective colonists, who built their own homes on them. Squatters living in caves along the riverbank refused to give up their caves when new landowners were ready to take over property they had purchased, so many of the new landowners also built caves along the Delaware River bank to live in until property rights were settled. The first houses they built were log cabins, much like those of earlier Swedish settlers.

William Penn's house was the first brick house built in the colonies, in 1682. Brick was preferred over wood because clay was plentiful in the area and doesn't burn.

THE FIRST CHILD

The first child of English parents born after the first English immigration to the New World was born in a cave in 1682. Later, the cave became the Pennypot Tavern. The child, John Key, was known as the "firstborn." He lived to the ripe old age of 85.

IMMIGRANTS ARRIVE IN PHILADELPHIA FIRST

The Port of Philadelphia was the primary entry point for immigrants to all the colonies, and many remained here because of the good farming land nearby. To accommodate the immigrants, many property owners constructed tenements, or small houses at the rear of their property, to rent out. The first tenements were built by George Mifflin at 742-46 South Front Street (look for his initials and the date—1748—in the brick), and they are still used today for housing.

Mifflin sold the houses to John Workman, who added properties and built a courtyard. The Workman family owned these houses until 1906. By that time, the area had become a slum, populated by new immigrants. The houses were then purchased by an advocate of housing reform, Lydia S. Clark, and later taken over by the Octavia Hill Association, which operated them as rental properties.

The First Town Houses

Row houses were symbolic of Philadelphia before we knew they were "town houses." The need for housing, as more immigrants arrived, became urgent. In 1799, William Sansom built the first complete row of homes. He designed 22 houses on the 700 block of Walnut Street, followed by 20 houses on Sansom Street a few years later. The design was simple because the units were identical. Sansom paved the street at his expense in order to entice tenants to come all the way to the outskirts of the city, as Sansom Street was then.

SHOOTING MORE THAN STARS

Sparks' Shot Tower, built in 1808, was the first and tallest tower of its kind in the United States. It was built at 29-31 Carpenter Street by makers of leaden vessels to manufacture shot for sport. The manufacturing process was simple: Molten lead was poured through perforated pans at the top of this 142-foot tower. In its descent, the lead spun into droplets, which hardened when they hit cold water at the bottom.

The tower became a munitions factory during the War of 1812. Sparks' continued to produce shot for sport until 1907. The tower, now sealed off, is located at a recreation center.

WATER, WATER

The first municipal waterworks in the nation became one of the most important and unusual engineering accomplishments of its time. The original steam pumping station carried about four million gallons of water from the Schuylkill River to reservoirs at the present site of the Philadelphia Museum of Art. There, the water was gravity-fed to homes and hydrants.

The west facade of Fairmount Water Works from the locks of the Schuylkill Navigation Company, circa 1865. *Courtesy of the Philadelphia Water Department, Water Works Interpretive Center, c. 1865, from stereoview by J. Moran*

As the city population increased, more water was needed and the system was refined, with additions modeled after Roman temples and arranged around paved courts and walkways. The water pumping machinery was so state-of-the-art that galleries were opened inside for visitors. The grounds were carefully landscaped and later became part of Fairmount Park.

LEMON HILL

In 1844, the city purchased Lemon Hill, an estate along the Schuylkill on which a Federal-style home built by Robert Morris in 1774 once stood, to protect the municipal water supply. Morris had sold the estate to Henry Pratt, who built the house that still exists on the site. Lemon Hill became the first part of Fairmount Park in 1855.

Water Needed to Match Growth

At first, in 1801, water was pumped to a neoclassical tower at Centre Square, but this process soon became obsolete. The site for the new waterworks was blasted out of rock at the foot of Fair Mount, as the area was called then and where the Art Museum is now. Although it initially ran on steam engines, the cost for fuel for the pumping mechanism grew too expensive, so engineers built the world's longest dam to move the water naturally. This was considered the greatest technological feat of its time. By the middle of the 19th century, city reservoirs were being emptied twice a week, and it was clear that as elegant as the waterworks were, they had become inadequate.

Increasing city population and pollution of the Delaware made it clear that more sophisticated equipment in new facilities was essential to supply the city's need and purify the delivery system. In 1812, work was started on the new, improved, and expanded system. The waterworks were an unprecedented engineering accomplishment, attracting tourists from across the country and as far away as Europe. Because of the waterworks, the city bought land along the Schuylkill and Wissahickon watersheds to keep industry out so that the water supply would stay pure. This city-owned open space became Fairmount Park.

Pollution: An Old Issue

But industrial chemicals and other pollution coming from upstream communities meant the end of using the Schuylkill River for drinking water, and the waterworks were abandoned in 1909. An aquarium was installed there in 1911, with 1,500 fish and a giant loggerhead turtle named Dover. The aquarium closed in 1960, and this 183-year-old National Historic Landmark is once again slated for renovation and restoration.

FIRST IN ACOUSTICS

When the Academy of Music was built, it sat without a roof for a year to allow the walls to settle. Five years before it opened, a fund-raising drive had been organized that raised $400,000. When it was finally completed in 1857, the building's acoustics were unsurpassed.

The first opera performed at the Academy was *Il Trovatore*. King Edward VII visited the hall when he was Prince of Wales, as did Dom Pedro, emperor of Brazil, while attending the Centennial Exhibition. Today, it is the oldest musical auditorium in the country still serving its original function.

Broad Street Was Quiet Then

When the Academy's site at Broad and Locust Streets was selected, Broad Street was a quiet, undeveloped location. The architects, Napoleon LeBrun and Gustave Runge, selected through a competition, modeled the performance hall after La Scala, in Milan. The interior is designed like a huge barrel. The ceiling balloons out in a dome, and the rear walls of the auditorium are curved. A well was excavated beneath the parquet, or main floor, and a sounding board was placed in the orchestra pit. The huge crystal chandelier that pulls every eye toward its splendor was originally in the old Crystal Palace in New York City. To prevent it from falling, it hangs from a separate iron structure above the ceiling, suspended by several cables. The Academy hosted a grand ball, which surpassed any event held in the city until that time, to celebrate its opening.

APARTMENTS IN THE PARK

Alden Park, at Wissahickon Avenue and School House Lane, is a familiar sight to Philadelphians as they turn onto Lincoln Drive. Built in 1920, this was the first apartment complex in the country built in a park-like setting. The developer, Lawrence Jones, wanted to build luxury apartments for families who liked the convenience of being near Center City but wanted to live in a country-like setting without home maintenance responsibilities.

The recent proliferation of co-ops and condos is testimony to Jones' progressive thinking. The complex of three buildings sits on 30 acres overlooking the Wissahickon Valley. Originally, the luxurious complex had a nine-hole golf course, a year-round swimming pool, formal gardens, and individual garden plots for green-thumb residents.

MORE FIRSTS

☆ The **first statue built with public funds** was erected in 1809 in Centre Square, at the site of the early waterworks and where City Hall is now located. Known as the Nymph of the Schuylkill, its official title was *Water Nymph and Bittern*, and it was sculpted by artist William Rush. When the waterworks were moved and Centre Square was demolished, the nymph was moved indoors to the new waterworks at Fair Mount. She stayed there until the pumping station was removed. Because the original sculpture was made of wood, the nymph didn't have a long life. She was recast in bronze and is now in the American wing of the Philadelphia Museum of Art. All that remains of the original is the wooden head, somewhere in a private collection.

☆ Robert Mills was the **first native-born American architect**. In 1809, he constructed a row of houses called Franklin Row on South Eighth Street on speculation. His designs were influenced by the neoclassical ideas of Thomas Jefferson and Benjamin Latrobe.

☆ Thomas Ustick Walter, a mason who was apprenticed to famous architect and engineer William Strickland, was a founder of the **first professional organization of architects**, the American Institute of Architects, in 1867.

☆ Benjamin Chew Tighman invented **sandblasting**, the process of cleaning, engraving, cutting, and boring glass, stone, or metal with pressurized sand. The year was 1870.

☆ The **revolving door** was designed and first built by Theophilus Van Kannel of Philadelphia, who patented his invention in 1888. He called it a "storm door structure."

Amen!

OLDEST CHURCH

In 1638, the first group of Swedish settlers came to the Delaware Valley. They hired Peter Minuit, the Dutchman who had engineered the Manhattan land deal, as guide and leader, and established themselves along the Delaware River, preceding William Penn.

The settlers' first chapel, built in 1645, was fairly primitive. It was made of logs, with loopholes so that the settlers could spy and shoot attacking Indians. (Fortunately, their relationship with their Native American neighbors improved considerably by the end of the century—so much so that the colonists translated the Lutheran Catechism into the Leni Lenape language in hopes of winning the tribe over to Christianity.)

In 1698, the settlers laid the cornerstone for Old Swedes' Church (Gloria Dei) on the site of their old log cabin chapel. All construction was paid for by the worshippers. The belfry was left unfinished, to see how God would provide for it. He, or She, did, because eventually, the belfry was completed.

LET LIGHTNING NOT STRIKE

One of the earliest lightning rod systems in the world was installed on the exterior of Gloria Dei Church. Nils Collin, the pastor sent from Sweden to serve the congregation, was a good friend of Benjamin Franklin's.

Gloria Dei (Old Swedes')
Episcopal Church, built for and
by the early Swedish settlers,
constructed between 1698 and
1700. The church was designated
a National Historic Site in 1942.
Courtesy of Gloria Dei Church

Gloria Dei is the oldest church in continuous use in America, and possibly the oldest building in Philadelphia. The baptismal font, which came from the Old Country with the early colonists, is still in use. Justus Falckner, the first Lutheran pastor of Old Swedes', was the first minister of any denomination to be ordained in the colonies.

Swedes Become Episcopalian

Until the American Revolution, pastors came from Sweden to minister to Swedish colonists, but by the end of the war, the Swedish congregations in the colonies began electing their own clergy. Gloria Dei, originally part of the Lutheran Mission, joined the Episcopal Communion after acquiring its own pastor in 1845. Eventually, all the Swedish congregations followed suit and joined the Episcopal Church. The Lutheran communities all spoke German at this time, and the Swedes felt more at home with the English-speaking Episcopalians.

FROM PORTUGAL AND SPAIN TO PHILADELPHIA

Congregation Mikveh Israel's roots go back to 1740, when a small group of Spanish-Portuguese Jews gathered to worship together. Mikveh Israel is responsible for many firsts in Philadelphia's Jewish community. A number of its founders were descendants of refugees from the Spanish Inquisition. Members included Haym Salomon, a financier of the Revolutionary War; Nathan Levy, whose ship *The Myrtilla* brought the Liberty Bell to this country; and Rebecca Gratz, philanthropist, early social worker and educator, and member of an illustrious Jewish Philadelphia family.

An interior view of the first Jewish religious assembly in Pennsylvania, Congregation Mikveh Israel. *Courtesy of Congregation Mikveh Israel*

CHRISTIANS HELP JEWS

Members of Christ Church contributed to the founding of Congregation Mikveh Israel, and the public subscription list was signed by Benjamin Franklin, Benjamin Rush, and David Rittenhouse.

Slow Beginnings

Before the congregation grew large enough to have its synagogue, a group of Jews worshipped in a small house in Sterling Alley. Records show that John Penn, proprietor of Pennsylvania, deeded a land grant to Nathan Lane for a "burial ground for several Jews." But it wasn't until 1780 that the first Jewish religious assembly in Pennsylvania was formally organized, and Congregation Mikveh Israel was officially founded.

Gershom Mendes Seixas was Mikveh Israel's first rabbi; he was the only rabbi of the synagogue, right up to this day, to be born in the United States. He came from a family of Portuguese emigrés. Rabbi Seixas, a devout patriot, was one of 14 clergymen who participated in George Washington's inauguration.

Mikveh Israel is responsible for initiating the first Hebrew Sunday school in America, today called the Hebrew Sunday School Society, as well as Gratz College, the first Hebrew teachers college in the Western Hemisphere.

HEBREW TEACHING COLLEGE

Gratz College was endowed by Mikveh Israel congregant Hyman Gratz. He included a codicil in his will calling for the "establishment and support of a college for the education of Jews residing in the city and county of Philadelphia."

The college opened in 1897, but when private funding became a problem, Gratz College joined with the Hebrew Education Society. Together they developed a curriculum designed to provide teachers of Hebrew with adequate education. A normal school (i.e., teachers college) was established to prepare teachers for Sunday religious schools, and in 1945 Gratz College set up a graduate degree program. The college offers programs in an academic setting, and focuses on Judaic studies for religious teachers and students. The liberal arts curriculum includes subjects such as sociology and literature. In addition to the college program, Jewish education classes are conducted for students from elementary through high school.

Rebecca Gratz

Jewish educator Rebecca Gratz founded the Hebrew Sunday School Society in 1838. Before she was 20, Gratz helped run a private welfare agency, the Female Association for the Relief of Women and Children in Reduced Circumstances; she was also a founding member of the Philadelphia Orphan Asylum. Her major role in founding the Hebrew Benevolent Society, an independent agency, started the network of Jewish charitable organizations in Philadelphia today. Legend has it that Washington Irving described Gratz's beauty to Sir Walter Scott, who then based Rebecca, the heroine of *Ivanhoe*, on her.

Ashkenazic Synagogue

Rodeph Shalom Synagogue is the oldest Ashkenazic (Central European) Jewish congregation in the Western world, founded in Philadelphia in 1795. By that year, there was enough of a Jewish population in Philadelphia that wanted to pray "according to German and Dutch rules," without the confines of the rituals of Mikveh Israel. This quotation appeared in Article 1 of the Articles of Association adopted by the German

Hebrew Society in 1810 and chartered by the Commonwealth of Pennsylvania on August 12, 1812. The German Hebrew Society was the genesis of Rodeph Shalom as a Reform congregation (although it began as an Orthodox one).

Philadelphia was the only city in the States in the 18th century to have two synagogues, as well as the first American city to have an Ashkenazic place of worship. In 1866, famous Philadelphia architect Frank Furness designed Rodeph Shalom's first building, a Moorish-style synagogue on North Broad Street. By 1926 the congregation had outgrown these facilities, and a new building was dedicated two years later. Today, a suburban branch exists as well.

FROM ANGLICAN TO EPISCOPALIAN

During the Revolutionary War, it was difficult for Anglican clergy to support the cause for independence, as they had sworn an oath of allegiance to the Crown and the English liturgy. Those clergy who remained loyal to their homeland returned to England; others, sympathetic to the cause of independence, remained.

CHRIST CHURCH ATTRACTS PATRIOTS

Seven signers of the Declaration of Independence were members of Christ Church, a part of Philadelphia history since 1695. In 1696, a frame structure was erected at Second and Church Streets and paved inside with brick. Eventually, a new church was built on the same site as the original. Buried in its cemetery are Benjamin and Deborah Franklin, as well as the other Declaration signers. Other parishioners included the Penn family, George Washington, the Marquis de Lafayette, and Betsy Ross.

Christ Church, the first Protestant Episcopal Church, represents the unity of those Christians who reorganized the Anglican Church in America after the Revolutionary War by expressing their loyalty to a wholly American clergy.
Courtesy of Christ Church

Conflicted Loyalties Divide the Church

The Anglican churches in the new nation lost almost half their clergy after the signing of the Declaration of Independence because of these mixed loyalties. When the Reverend Jacob Duché left for England in 1777 as a Loyalist, his assistant, William White, succeeded him as rector of the United Churches of Christ Church, St. Peter's, and St. James'.

White had no dual loyalties, and served as spiritual leader for the Founding Fathers. He wrote a pamphlet urging that, as ties with England had been broken, the churches were free to decide on unification or separation. This pamphlet made him the focus of church reorganization, and by the time the Treaty of Paris was signed in 1783, the Episcopal churches in the new nation had a plan for reorganization. White, who was consecrated as a bishop in 1787, helped reorganize the Anglican Church in America at Christ Church as the Protestant Episcopal Church of the United States.

EARLY AFRICAN AMERICAN EPISCOPALIANS

The Free African Society was formed on May 17, 1787, by the Reverend Absalom Jones and the Reverend Richard Allen to provide support in sickness and to benefit widows and fatherless children. The organization's name was changed to the African Friendly Society after the establishment, in 1793, of the first black Protestant Episcopal church in the country—the African Episcopal Church of St. Thomas. This church, the first African American parish of the Episcopal Church, joined the Diocese of Pennsylvania in 1794, under Jones' leadership. Jones, who had been born into slavery in 1746, was the first black Protestant Episcopal priest, and led his congregation for more than 24 years. He was ordained as a deacon in 1795 and as a priest in 1804 by Bishop White.

The Reverends Jones and Allen had been lay preachers at St. George's Methodist Episcopal Church, which had a large percentage of black parishioners. In a movement to separate the black Methodists from the white church because of racial discrimination, the African Methodist Episcopal Church was established. Its first general convention was held April 9–11, 1816, when Allen was ordained as the first bishop.

ABSALOM JONES AS MASONIC LEADER

The Reverend Absalom Jones was installed as the First Worshipful Master of the Lodge when the first African Masonic Lodge of Philadelphia was warranted in 1797. He was installed by Grand Master Prince Hall. Jones was also elected First Grand Master of the First Independent African Grand Lodge of Pennsylvania in 1815.

GIVE TO THE POOR

It was, after all, William Penn's "Holy Experiment," which welcomed all religions in a non-meddlesome spirit, that got so many immigrants to flock to Philadelphia. In 1701, Penn issued the Charter of Privileges, commemorated at Welcome Park, which invited people of all faiths to live comfortably in the City of Brotherly Love.

Religious freedom is a tenet of the Quakers, and so is charity. The first almshouse was established by the Society of Friends in 1713 for the care of indigent Quakers. Almost 20 years later, in 1732, the city opened the first municipal almshouse. The Philadelphia Almshouse, in addition to serving the poor, operated a hospital for the sick and insane. Located at Third and Spruce Streets, this hospital was the forerunner of Philadelphia General Hospital.

CATHOLICS FIND A HOME

William Penn was willing to accept Catholics in his new city, but he wanted them to practice their religion in secret and not make waves about it. St. Joseph's was the first Roman Catholic Church in Philadelphia, established in 1730 in Willing's Alley, a well-hidden place. Catholics often worshipped outside the city limits, in small, out-of-the-way chapels, whose real function was disguised behind store fronts and houses. This didn't sit well back home, and letters of complaint went back to clergy in England decrying the "Propagation of Papery abroad."

Catholics Get Bolder

Once Catholics could practice their religion openly, they began to establish Catholic schools. Roman Catholic High School for Boys, opened in Philadelphia in 1890, was the first free Catholic secondary school in America, the gift of Thomas E. Cahill. Cahill left a bequest for the purchase of ground and a building for the education of boys under the direction of the archdiocese. This marked the opening of the diocesan high school structure, with its emphasis on religious studies that made it different from any secondary school development in the world.

Catholic colleges were next. The Newman Club movement, so much a part of the life of Catholic college students throughout the country, was started in Philadelphia in October 1893 by a group of medical and dental students at the University of Pennsylvania, led by Timothy L. Harrington of Wisconsin, a medical student at Penn. Father J. P. Garvey, rector of the University Parish, St. James' Church, was spiritual director of the group. On March 29, 1894, Dr. William Pepper, the university provost, attended a reception to gain campus recognition of the Newman Club.

PHILADELPHIA PRODUCES A SAINT

Born in 1811 in Bohemia, John Neumann came to Philadelphia, then the largest diocese in the United States, in 1852 as the city's fourth bishop. He was declared a saint in 1977, the third American citizen to be canonized, and the first American man.

As a young student in Eastern Europe preparing for ordination, Neumann was determined to be a missionary in America, and he applied to be admitted to the Philadelphia Diocese. After service in New York State, Pittsburgh, and Baltimore, he was called to Philadelphia by the Pope.

The First Redemptorist

He was attracted to an order called "Redemptorist," and was the first novice of that order in America, as well as the first to be professed, or to declare his intent to be a Redemptorist. At age 31, he made his profession as a member of the Congregation of the Most Holy Redeemer in Baltimore.

In 1852, Pope Pius IX appointed Neumann the fourth bishop of Philadelphia, where he established the first system of Catholic parochial

Saint John Neumann, fourth bishop of Philadelphia from 1852 to 1860. *Courtesy of the National Shrine of Saint John Neumann*

schools in the United States, added many churches to the diocese, and introduced the practice of Forty Hours' Devotion on a regular schedule, a practice which eventually spread throughout the nation. (Forty Hours' Devotion is three days of veneration for the Blessed Sacrament, a thanksgiving for the Lord's presence in the form of bread and wine. It generally begins Sunday after Mass and continues for three days, or 40 hours.)

After Neumann's death in 1860 and his entombment in the basement chapel of St. Peter's Church, visitors to his burial site began to speak of miraculous cures after touching his casket, which they attributed to his intercession. However, no miracles were recorded until 1923. Preliminary steps were introduced in Rome regarding Neumann's sanctity. He is the first male in the American Church hierarchy to be canonized.

MYSTICS ALONG THE WISSAHICKON

A group of devout and mystic hermits from Germany settled in caves and log cabins in 71 acres of wilderness along the Wissahickon River. Their leader was Johannes Kelpius, the site was called Kelpius' cave, and the earliest known date of their settlement was 1694. Kelpius referred to his "home" as "Burrow of Rocks," the genesis of "Roxborough."

THE FUTURE FORETOLD

In predicting horoscopes, the mystics were not so different from the educated men of their time. Calculating the position of the stars, they determined future careers and auspicious times for travel, marriage, and business enterprises.

The hermits dabbled in astrology, fortune-telling, and some magic, and they liked to discuss mystifying passages in the Bible, particularly the 12th chapter of the Book of Revelations. They spoke and wrote of the coming of "the woman of the wilderness," who is mentioned in that chapter, and they acquired the group name Society of the Woman of the Wilderness. This group of Pietists, who considered themselves Rosicrucians, were known by other names as well: Hermits of the Mystic Brotherhood and Hermits of the Ridge.

SEAMEN PRAY ON WATER

The Seamen's Church Institute began in 1849 as the first—and only—floating church. The Floating Chapel of the Redeemer was a barge that floated down the Delaware River to provide religious services for sailors. The Right

The Floating Chapel of the Redeemer, literally located on the water, floated down the Delaware River and initiated the Seamen's Church Institute. *Courtesy of the Seamen's Church Institute*

Reverend Alonze Potter consecrated the church, and regular Sunday services were held. The mission work was later transferred to quarters on land, and in 1878, to the Church of the Redeemer. Eventually, this became an interdenominational society to provide a wide range of services to seamen.

FOR SAILORS ONLY

The first church in the world for seamen was built in Philadelphia in 1820 and led by the Reverend Robert Eastburn. It was known as the Mariner's Bethel.

Still in existence and now called the Seamen's Church Institute and the Apostleship of the Sea, the organization satisfies the spiritual and material needs of foreign seamen who dock in Philadelphia, often on ships from all around the world. The society offers services to sailors on all ships that enter the Port of Philadelphia. These include wiring money, sending packages home, shopping, and ministering. It also provides holiday dinners, gifts, and a warm welcome in an unfamiliar place.

MORE FIRSTS

☆ **Baptists established themselves** in Philadelphia before the first city charter. In 1688, five Baptists from Wales, along with seven others, organized the Pennypack Baptist Church.

☆ The **first presbytery of the Presbyterian Church** in the United States was formed in Philadelphia in 1705, composed of seven ministers from Philadelphia, Maryland, Delaware, and the eastern shore of Virginia.

☆ The **first Mennonite church in America** was built in Germantown, and its first service was held on May 23, 1708.

☆ The **oldest Methodist Episcopal church in America** is St. George's United Methodist Church, built in 1769. Methodist ideas came to Philadelphia via Dr. Joseph Pilmoor, who preached his first sermon from the steps of the State House. The first meetings were held in Loxley's Court, between Arch and Cherry Streets. The church was purchased from Dutch settlers as an unfinished building, and it remained without floors up until Revolutionary times.

☆ The **first Roman Catholic church for Germans** was organized in 1787, with articles of incorporation granted on October 4, 1788. It was called the Church of the Holy Trinity in the City of Philadelphia.

☆ The **first orphan society in the United States**, the Roman Catholic Society of St. Joseph for Educating and Maintaining Poor Orphan Children, was organized by the Reverend Leonard Neale in 1806.

☆ The **first Bible society**, the Bible Society of Philadelphia, was founded on December 12, 1808. In 1840, its name was changed to the Pennsylvania Bible Society.

☆ The **first Jewish chaplain of the U.S. Army** was the Reverend Jacob Frankel of Philadelphia, who was appointed on September 18, 1862. When his chaplaincy was over, he was reassigned to the United States Hospital in this city.

Ethnic Pride

SWEDES—FIRST EUROPEAN SETTLERS IN PENNSYLVANIA

The idea of settling in the New World was proposed to the Swedish monarch in the 1620s by the Dutch West India Company, but the Thirty Years' War began and that was that—for a while. The Dutch persisted and persuaded the Swedish queen's minister to establish a Swedish settlement. New Sweden, as it was called, was set up in the Delaware Valley in 1638, before the arrival of William Penn. It was the site of the first permanent European settlement in the area. New Sweden was not intended to be a colony, but rather an outpost for the commercial trade of the riches of the New World, like tobacco and furs.

A celebration of Midsommarfest at the American Swedish Historical Museum. *Photograph by Elin Rantakrans, courtesy of the American Swedish Historical Museum*

When settlers arrived in the New World, it was not uncommon for some of them to be given property by authorities back home; in those days, usually royalty. A land tract granted by original royal deed to a Swedish lieutenant, Sven Skute, in 1653 is now the site of the American Swedish Historical Museum, the oldest Swedish museum in the United States. Founded in 1926, its mission is to preserve Swedish and Swedish-American culture, heritage, and traditions. The museum preserves and exhibits Swedish contributions in history, art, architecture, music, science, and technology.

☞ To Visit: American Swedish Historical Museum

American Swedish Historical Museum
1900 Pattison Avenue
Philadelphia, PA 19145-5901
215-389-1776
Hours: Tuesday-Friday, 10 A.M.-4 P.M.; Saturday-Sunday, 12-4 P.M. Closed holidays.
Admission charged; children under 12 accompanied by an adult are admitted free.

FIRST AMERICAN JEWISH MUSEUM

The National Museum of American Jewish History is the first and only museum in the country that focuses solely on the American Jewish experience. It was designed to be part of the new home of Mikveh Israel, the oldest synagogue in the city, at a site north of Market between Fourth and Fifth Streets, where it would become part of Independence National Historical Park. The plans for the relocated synagogue included a chapel, a meeting room, and classrooms, as well as museum space. The museum was officially opened in July 1976, during the country's bicentennial. Both the National Museum of American Jewish History and the re-creation of the synagogue of the American Revolution now sit in the shadow of Independence Hall.

Although both institutions share the same building, their functions are separate. Mikveh Israel is a place of worship and study; the museum sponsors exhibits, lectures, and educational visits in conjunction with schools and other cultural organizations.

A PRAYER BOOK FOR AMERICANS

Isaac Leeser, spiritual leader of Congregation Mikveh Israel from 1829 to 1850, published the first Jewish prayer book in America and introduced the English sermon into the American synagogue. At the age of 28, he began a two-year project of translating the Sephardic (Spanish-Jewish) prayer book into English-Hebrew. The resulting work, *The Form of Prayers According to the Custom of the Spanish and Portuguese Jews*, appeared in 1837. It was considered a major contribution to American Jewish liturgical literature, as was *Leeser's Hebrew Reader* of 1838, the first juvenile Hebrew speller for Jews in the United States.

☞ *To Visit: National Museum of American Jewish History*

National Museum of American Jewish History
55 North Fifth Street, Independence Mall East
Philadelphia, PA 19106
215-923-3811
Hours: Monday-Thursday, 10 A.M.-5 P.M.; Friday, 10 A.M.-3 P.M.;
Sunday, 12-5 P.M.
Admission charged; children under 6 and members are admitted free.

Sculptor Sir Moses Jacob Ezekiel created *Religious Liberty* in 1876. The marble monument was exhibited at the Centennial Exhibition in Fairmount Park, was later relocated, and was rededicated in 1985 on the grounds of the National Museum of American Jewish History. *Courtesy of the National Museum of American Jewish History*

CITY SUPPORTS BLACK MUSEUM

The African American Museum in Philadelphia, established in 1976, was the first structure built by a major city in the United States to house and commemorate the life and work of African Americans. It serves as a focus of activity for black artists, musicians, and writers through exhibits, lectures, and special events. Collections document Negro League baseball, the careers of eminent African Americans, and other memorabilia pertinent to African American life.

Exhibits cover political, religious, and family life, as well as the civil rights movement, sports, art, and entertainment. The museum sponsors concerts, films, dance, poetry readings, and seminars. A contract with the city of New York schedules trips to the museum for New York school-children. The museum states as its mission: "To collect, preserve, interpret and present the lives and contributions of African Americans, primarily in, but not limited to, the Commonwealth of Pennsylvania and the Delaware Valley region."

☞ *To Visit: African American Museum in Philadelphia*

African American Museum in Philadelphia
701 Arch Street
Philadelphia, PA 19106
215-574-0380
Hours: Tuesday-Saturday, 10 A.M.-5 P.M.; Sunday, 12-6 P.M.
Closed national holidays and Good Friday.
Admission charged.

THE HOUSE THAT CULTURES BUILT

International House, established in 1910, is the first and oldest facility in the country that provides a haven for foreign students, as well as a cultural and educational center for Philadelphia.

A home as well as a house, the building includes living accommodations, film and folk culture programs, language instruction, and, more than anything, friendship. It all began in 1908 on the University of Pennsylvania campus when the Reverend A. Waldo Stevenson, recently returned from Cuba as a missionary, started to talk with a group of Chinese students about their loneliness, the inadequate housing, and the general unfriendliness of their environment. Stevenson invited the students to his home, and that home soon became a meeting place for many foreign students from all over the world. In a few years, it became clear that Stevenson's home was no longer adequate for the needs of the large foreign student population, and the Christian Association got involved. International House was the result.

A House Becomes a Home

By 1917, the association had acquired a building at 39th and Spruce Streets, which became the center for activities and provided living quarters for a few students. After several moves and through fund-raising campaigns, grants, and loans, the new International House opened at its present location in 1970, providing housing for both foreign and American students. Foreign students living there have the comfort of hearing their native language spoken, and American students appreciate the exposure to foreign cultures and languages. The public has the advantage of a great variety of music, art, film, dance, and exhibits from many cultures.

TRAINING MEANS JOBS; JOBS MEAN SECURITY

What started out as just a gleam in the Reverend Leon Sullivan's eye is now a vast network of programs that train disadvantaged people throughout the world so that they can rise out of economic deprivation. The Opportunities Industrialization Centers (OIC) started in Philadelphia, the first outreach organization of its kind in the country.

In the late 1950s, when he was pastor of Zion Baptist Church in North Philadelphia, Sullivan led a campaign to create thousands of jobs for African Americans in Philadelphia. But that was just the beginning. In 1962, Sullivan founded Progress Plaza Investment Associates, a savings cooperative that built the first and largest shopping center owned by blacks in a major urban area, still a thriving enterprise on North Broad Street. This was followed two years later by the OIC, a network of community-based training programs that produced millions of jobs in many cities. The program has grown internationally and now serves 18 countries through 33 centers in Africa, Asia, Eastern Europe, and Central America.

FIGHTING JOB DISCRIMINATION IN SOUTH AFRICA

The Sullivan Principles, a code of conduct for companies operating in South Africa and other parts of the world, have become a standard for social responsibility. These principles have been effective in fighting discrimination against blacks in the South African workplace and have provided a platform for the campaign for equal rights throughout that nation.

The Reverend Leon H. Sullivan, organizer of Opportunities Industrialization Centers, a worldwide avenue for self-determination.
Courtesy of Progress Plaza and OIC

OIC International, the outgrowth of Sullivan's Philadelphia initiative, works in developing countries to teach marketable skills to young men and women to improve their economic future and ensure their quality of life. The organization also offers job placement, assistance in small business development, and agricultural settlements.

MORE THAN THE ITALIAN MARKET

The first Italian Studies Center at any university in the country was founded at the University of Pennsylvania in 1978. Its work centers on coordinating concentrations in various disciplines that deal with Italian studies by integrating subjects that relate to the ancient and contemporary Italian world. The center sponsors conferences on subjects such as Italian cinema and Primo Levi and the Holocaust, which attract scholars and interested laypeople from the entire community.

A SURPRISING LEGACY

Mariano DiVito, an Italian immigrant who came to the United States in 1907 and became first a waiter and then maitre d' at the Bellevue Stratford Hotel, bequeathed $1,250,000 to the Italian Studies Center upon his death in 1987.

PRESBYTERIANS HARBOR THEIR HISTORY

The Presbyterian Historical Society is the nation's oldest denominational historical society, housing a library and archives at 425 Lombard Street in Philadelphia. The society is also known as the Department of History of the Presbyterian Church (USA).

The number of items housed in the society's headquarters is staggering: 200,000 published titles and 20 million manuscripts. Six statues by Alexander Calder in front of the building commemorate American Presbyterian personalities who were significant in the development of the Church. They represent Francis Makemie, sometimes called the "Father of Organized American Presbyterianism"; John Witherspoon, delegate to the Continental Congress and the only active clergyman to sign the Declaration of Independence; Samuel Davies, the fourth president of the College of New Jersey; James Caldwell, chaplain of Dayton's New Jersey Regiment in the Revolutionary War; Marcus Whitman, a physician missionary to Oregon whose trip opened part of the Oregon Trail; and John McMillan, the first settled Presbyterian minister in western Pennsylvania. Also on exhibit in the Presbyterian Historical Society are works by Rembrandt, James Peale, Bass Otis, and John Neagle. The headquarters serves all of the American Presbyterian and Reformed churches, and the building on Lombard Street is open to the public.

DOLLS REFLECT BLACK HISTORY

"They're not just dolls; they're history." That's how Barbara Whiteman, creator of the Philadelphia Doll Museum, the first museum to feature black dolls, describes her collection, Dark Images. Whiteman is the founder and executive director of the museum, which was established in 1988. Her 300 dolls range in size from miniature figurines to full-size dolls. She started her collection after realizing that black dolls are a fairly recent innovation, and she began tracing the connection between today, when there is a relative abundance of black dolls, and the past, when they were rare.

Almost as soon as she started collecting, Whiteman realized that black dolls reflect how blacks were perceived historically. Many dolls in the collection are homemade; they were constructed from all sorts of materials, ranging from chicken bones to bisque, an unglazed white ceramic. Her collection is used as a teaching tool: Whiteman visits schools and libraries, using the dolls as a means to teach African American history.

"Ayoka" is a modern doll created by artist Annette Hemstedt, and on exhibit at the Philadelphia Doll Museum. *Courtesy of Barbara Whiteman, Philadelphia Doll Museum*

☞ *To Visit: Philadelphia Doll Museum*

Philadelphia Doll Museum
2253 North Broad Street
Philadelphia, PA 19132
215-787-0220
Hours: Thursday-Saturday, 10 A.M.-4 P.M.; Sunday, 12-4 P.M.
Also by appointment.
Admission charged.

IN THE SPIRIT OF QUAKER SERVICE

The American Friends Service Committee (AFSC) was founded in 1917 by Philadelphia Quakers who, conscientious objectors themselves, wanted to provide all conscientious objectors with an alternative to active war duty during World War I. At the end of the war, AFSC supplied French farmers with seeds and livestock, planted fruit trees, and repaired machinery. In 1931, it distributed food to 40,000 children of unemployed coal miners in Appalachia.

The organization, still under Quaker sponsorship and still headquartered in Philadelphia, is committed to social justice, peace, and humanitarian service. Members of all faiths are welcome, and programs now exist in Africa, Asia, Latin America, and the Middle East, as well as in the United States.

Make Peace, Not War

At the outbreak of World War II, AFSC resumed its work with conscientious objectors, providing them with alternative service in hospitals, conservation programs, and training schools. More recently, its programs have helped the homeless, organized health and safety training for workers in Mexico who are exposed to dangerous chemicals, and raised funds for North Korean flood relief.

WOMEN'S SOLIDARITY

The Million Woman March, the first African American women's gathering of such magnitude, brought an avalanche of women, filled with a sense of joyous sisterhood, to the Benjamin Franklin Parkway on October 25, 1997. The early morning rain passed, and the weather cooperated as the day wore on, never dampening the spirit of friendship and unity that infused every activity.

Crowds of African American women gather on the Benjamin Franklin Parkway for the first Million Woman March. *Courtesy of Studio Forty*

Women from almost every state in the nation came to show their support for African Americans and, to paraphrase their mission statement, to set realistic tasks and objectives and find effective solutions to ensure stability of the family unit and individual lives "as we move forward as a people."

The masses of women who gathered along the Parkway listened to speeches, made new friends, and celebrated the opportunity to be together and to exchange information about their lives, their families, their jobs, their dreams, and their disappointments. Many women who participated in the march considered it a "spiritual journey."

MORE FIRSTS

☆ The **first organization of Scotsmen** was formed in December 1749, when a group living in Philadelphia organized the St. Andrew's Society at Philadelphia in Pennsylvania. Its purpose was to aid poor and distressed Scotsmen.

☆ The **first black doctor** was Philadelphian James Derham, who eventually settled in New Orleans sometime before 1790. He studied under Dr. Benjamin Rush.

☆ The **first African American company in the Union Army** was mustered in 1863 in Philadelphia.

☆ The **first American Catholic historical society** was organized on July 22, 1884, in Philadelphia and is the oldest of its kind in the United States. The American Catholic Historical Society continues to preserve and publish documentary sources of Catholic history in America and disseminates information on Catholic contributions to the history of this nation.

☆ *A Raisin in the Sun* by Lorraine Hansberry opened at the Walnut Street Theatre on January 26, 1959, and was **the first play written by an African American to win a Drama Critics Circle Award.**

Protecting the Public

FIGHTING FIRES

William Penn didn't want his city destroyed the way the Great Fire destroyed so much of London in 1666, so he designed wide streets for easy access and encouraged the use of brick and stone in building construction. Such good thinking on Penn's part probably prevented many a fire in this fair city. But when one did break out, there was no fire company to come to the rescue; it was up to the building's owner to put it out.

By 1696, householders were required to keep ladders and a bucket of water handy. Equipment was primitive but sufficient—until 1730, when a huge fire devastated Fishbourn Wharf, resulting in damages of $5,000.

First Volunteers

That year, a fire engine was purchased and housed near the Friends Meeting House on Front Street, but it was kept outdoors and neglected. In 1734, the city council ordered three London fire engines, 400 buckets, and 25 hooks in response to Benjamin Franklin's declaration in *The Pennsylvania Gazette* that it was time for the city to take control of fire fighting.

The Union Fire Company was established by Franklin in 1736, and it fought fires in Philadelphia for 84 years. It was the first volunteer fire organization in the world, and it became the model for many fire companies to come. Firefighters carried their water in heavy leather buckets and were responsible not just for quelling flames but also for protecting burning buildings from looters.

Two years later, Andrew Bradford, Franklin's printing rival, organized the Fellowship Fire Company, which was followed by the Hand-in-Hand Fire Company in 1742. By the mid-18th century there were more fire companies, which were often as much social organizations as groups of serious firefighters. Had you walked in on one of them, you probably would have seen firemen lounging, talking, and playing cards as they waited to spring into action at the first sound of the alarm.

FIRE BELLS RING OUT

In 1752, the Union and Hand-in-Hand fire companies together bought a large fire bell that could be heard throughout the city. Wells were dug and public pumps installed so that water could be obtained quickly for fire fighting. By 1764, several fire companies had joined forces and had begun organizing into what would eventually be a citywide cooperative unit.

LET THERE BE LIGHT—AND PAVING

The first street lights in North America, illuminated by whale oil, were placed near Philadelphia front doors and businesses by individuals until 1751. In that year, the city installed its own street lighting system at the urging of its citizens.

A special tax was collected to pay for these lamps, which at first were imported from England. Globular in shape and fragile, they belched soot after a few hours' use. Benjamin Franklin redesigned them with four flat panes, a funnel to draw the smoke up, and a hole at the bottom to create a draft for the burning wick. These worked much better. The street lights had an added advantage: according to historians, they curtailed criminal activity after dark.

Cobblestones and Paving

Merchants took the initiative of installing cobblestones or paving blocks on the streets in front of their businesses until the city assumed that responsibility in 1762, with money collected through taxes and lotteries. Before the city took over this task (the first in the colonies to do so), citizens had been required by ordinance to spend several days a year doing road work—unless they paid a fee in lieu of actual labor. Newly appointed street commissioners supervised the paving of more than 120,000 square yards of streets and arranged to remove street rubbish on a weekly basis. A night watch was on the lookout for fires. The city was coming into its own.

ANCHORS AWEIGH

During the American Revolution, ships were built on the Delaware River. Philadelphia shipyards had already been building a variety of merchant ships, so it was relatively easy for them to switch to building warships when the time came. In 1775, designs for the first 12 frigates of the Continental Navy were prepared here. Following the ratification of the Constitution, the first two frigates, the *United States* and the *Constitution*, were built, and the United States Navy came into existence.

These frigates were designed and built by shipbuilder Joshua Humphreys, whose shipyard was south of Christian Street in the Southwark area of the city. After the frigate *Philadelphia* was launched, the secretary of the Navy acquired land to build an official navy yard near the foot of Wharton Street. The first navy yard was established in 1800, occupying about 12 acres from Prime Street (now Washington Avenue) to Wharton Street, from Front Street to the Delaware River. Thirty-five warships were built there between 1815 and 1875.

The Philadelphia Navy Yard

The property was sold in 1875 and the Philadelphia Naval Shipyard was moved to League Island, where the Delaware and Schuylkill Rivers meet. The land had been purchased by the city in 1862 for $310,000, and was presented to the federal government as a modern, state-of-the-art navy yard, although the Navy also built vessels and maintained storage facilities at two other locations—the Schuylkill Arsenal and the Frankford Arsenal.

Bigger—but Not Better!

The largest ship in the world, the USS *Pennsylvania*, was launched in July 1837, attracting almost 100,000 spectators to its christening. It took 15 years to build, and was the most heavily armed man-of-war ever designed. The ship was christened by Commodore James Biddle; he smashed a bottle of Pennsylvania whiskey and an aged bottle of Madeira on her figurehead. But the USS *Pennsylvania* took so long to build that by the time she was complete, she was already obsolete. Her longest, and only, sea journey was to the Norfolk Navy Yard, where she was burned in 1861 to prevent her capture by Confederates!

R AND R

During the Civil War, Union troops enjoyed the Union Volunteer Refreshment Saloon and Hospital, located next to navy yard ship houses. It was similar to what we later called the USO.

Father of the Navy

Almost everybody's heard of Commander John Paul Jones, but it's Commodore John Barry who bears the title "Father of the American Navy." Born in Ireland in 1745, he fought the last naval battle of the American Revolution aboard the frigate *Alliance* in 1783. His first command came in 1766, on the schooner *Barbados*, which sailed out of Philadelphia. Barry adopted the city as his home port, not only because it was becoming a major maritime center but also because he had more freedom to practice his Roman Catholic religion in this city than any other place in the colonies.

Commodore John Barry, considered the "Father of the American Navy," held the record for the fastest day of sailing in the 18th century. *Courtesy of Independence National Historical Park Collection*

Barry sailed many merchant ships between Philadelphia and the West Indies, but one of his biggest claims to fame was when he piloted back from England a ship owned by a friend, financier Robert Morris. He sailed 237 miles in a 24-hour period—the fastest day of sailing recorded in the 18th century.

NO TRAITOR HE

Commodore John Barry was approached by British sympathizers and offered a bribe and a commission in the Royal Navy if he would turn the ship he was then commanding, the *Effingham*, over to the British. He was indignant at the suggestion of becoming a turncoat and "spurned the eyedee of being a treater [*sic*]."

Barry's initial duty in the Revolutionary War was to outfit the first Continental Navy ships, which left the Port of Philadelphia. He was then commissioned a captain in the Continental Navy and given command of his first warship, the *Lexington*.

OLD SAILORS GET A HOME

The U.S. Naval Home was the first institution to provide a safe harbor for elderly, retired, or disabled naval and marine corps officers. In 1799, Congress voted to contribute money to a hospital fund, and naval personnel paid a small monthly charge—20 cents. The Pemberton Plantation, at Gray's Ferry Avenue and Bainbridge Street, was purchased in 1826, and construction of the Naval Home began in 1830. First called the Naval

Asylum, it opened in 1831 with four residents. The facility was also used as a naval school for midshipmen, directed by Commodore James Biddle. When naval education was transferred to Annapolis, the Asylum became known as the U.S. Naval Home.

FIRST U.S. CAVALRY

There were no official troops designated to defend colonial Philadelphia, so the all-volunteer "Light Horse," or cavalry, was established on November 17, 1774, at Carpenters' Hall. Most volunteers were members of the Gloucester Fox Hunting Club, the Friendly Sons of St. Patrick, and the Fishing Company of the State in Schuylkill, Philadelphia's elite social clubs. The Light Horse of the Cavalry of Philadelphia, as it was officially called, was later renamed the First Troop Philadelphia City Cavalry. It is the oldest mounted military unit in continuous service in the U.S. armed forces. Its members have served in every conflict from the Revolution onward.

First Troop Philadelphia City Cavalry escorts President Franklin Delano Roosevelt on February 22, 1936, at North Philadelphia Station. *Courtesy of Archives, First Troop Philadelphia City Cavalry*

Riding High

Today, the unit is part of the Pennsylvania Army National Guard, a troop of armored cavalry officially known as "A Troop, 1st Squadron, 104th Cavalry of the Pennsylvania Army National Guard." It rides in parades, and in army tanks when on National Guard duty. Preceding and during the Revolutionary War, the troop provided reconnaissance for the army and protected General George Washington's bodyguard. It escorted Washington from Philadelphia to Cambridge when he was commander in chief, and the troop has continued to escort presidents on various occasions ever since.

DISTINGUISHED VETERANS

First Troop Philadelphia City Cavalry has contributed many distinguished men to American history. Astronaut Charles Conrad, commander of *Apollo 12* and member of Sky Lab, and Thomas S. Gates, former secretary of defense and secretary of the Navy under President Eisenhower, were Troopers. So was John Dunlop, the printer of the Declaration of Independence.

First Troop's museum has an extensive collection of uniforms, memorabilia, and weapons from the Revolutionary period to the present. Its most treasured piece is the original troop standard, presented by the troop's first captain, Abraham Markoe, in 1775. The flag has 13 alternating blue and white stripes and the troop crest. Troopers claim that the "Markoe Standard" is the earliest surviving example of 13 stripes on an American banner. It was carried in all engagements until 1800, and is now on view in a special case.

☞ To Visit: First Troop Philadelphia City Cavalry Museum

First Troop Philadelphia City Cavalry Museum
The Armory
23rd and Ranstead Streets
Philadelphia, PA 19103
215-564-1488
Open to visitors by appointment.

THE MARINES LANDED IN A TAVERN

The U.S. Marine Corps was organized at Tun Tavern, once at the intersection of Front, Water, and King Streets, in 1775, by a resolution passed by the Continental Congress. The resolution, sponsored by John Adams, stated that "two Battalions of Marines be raised" as landing forces with the naval fleet.

The Continental Marines distinguished themselves almost immediately in their first amphibious raid on the Bahamas in March 1776. Their commander, Captain Samuel Nicholas, was the first commissioned officer in the Continental Marines, and he remained the senior officer throughout the Revolution. At the end of the Revolutionary War, the Continental Navy and Marines were dissolved, as mandated by the Treaty of Paris, in April 1783. But the Marine Corps was reestablished on July 11, 1798.

A tablet was installed on Water Street between Chestnut and Walnut commemorating the U.S. Marines. It read:

> This tablet marks the site of Tun Tavern, the birthplace of the
> United States Marine Corps. Here in 1775 Captain Samuel
> Nicholas, the first marine officer, opened a recruiting ren-
> dezvous for the marine battalions authorized by Resolution of
> the Continental Congress November 10, 1775.

The site was later destroyed to make way for Interstate 95.

THE CAISSONS GO ROLLING ALONG

The year 1775 was a big one in the creation of the U.S. Army and its component branches, and it all happened in Philadelphia. The Armor branch, organized on December 12, 1775, traces its origins to the cavalry, a regiment authorized by the Continental Congress.

The United States Army came into being on June 14, 1774, when the Continental Congress authorized the enlistment of riflemen to serve the colonies for one year. Ten companies of riflemen were authorized. The oldest regular army infantry regiment, the third, was constituted on June 3, 1784, as the First American Regiment. The post of adjutant general was established on the same date, and has been held continuously since then. Other army positions and divisions followed in due course. The Continental Congress authorized the post of chief engineer of the army on June 16, 1775, and on November 17 of that year it named a colonel of the regiment of artillery, electing Henry Knox to supervise artillery and field artillery. The Army Corps of Engineers was authorized by Congress on March 11, 1779.

MORE FIRSTS

☆ The **first society to offer charity to families of naval personnel** was started on July 4, 1765, in Philadelphia. It was called the Captains of Ships Charitable Club for Relief of Poor and Distressed Masters of Ships, their Widows and Children.

☆ The **first officers candidate school** was established at 1210 Chestnut Street during the Civil War.

☆ The **first training school for future officers of the United States Merchant Marine** was called the Pennsylvania Nautical School and was established on April 17, 1889, for young men ages 17 to 20. Their training ship was the U.S. sloop of war *Saratoga*, their "school" from 1890 to 1907.

Into the 21st Century with Science and Technology

THE FIRST COMPUTER

We may not know a modem from a mouse, but we do know all our reservations, bank business, telephone lines, and catalog ordering are dependent on computers, technology that has invaded everyone's life.

It all started at the University of Pennsylvania, more than 50 years ago, with a giant computer named ENIAC—an acronym for Electronic Numerical Integrator and Computer. This primitive giant, super-high-tech for its time, was no competition for the incredibly efficient and overwhelmingly competent computer that is an integral part of our lives today. Yet ENIAC, with all of its elementary qualities, was crucial to the future of computer technology.

Little more than a sophisticated calculator, this electronic marvel had to be manually wired to execute a program, and it was unable to store programs in its memory. It was 150 feet in width and had 20 banks of flashing lights.

GETTING THE BUGS OUT

Occasionally, an inquisitive flying bug wandered into the laboratory, inadvertently landing on ENIAC and short-circuiting the program. Hence, when something goes wrong with a computer today we say it has developed a "bug."

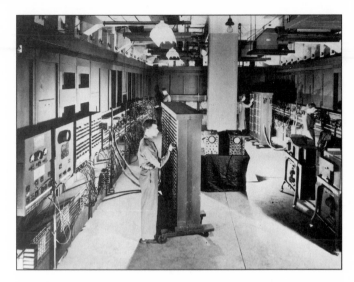

Compare this huge room filled with electronic equipment with the computers of today, and you see how far we've come from ENIAC, the first computer, developed at the School of Engineering at the University of Pennsylvania. *Courtesy of the Free Library of Philadelphia*

The Moore School building at the University of Pennsylvania's School of Engineering and Applied Science was the birthing room of the computer; the university had been assigned ballistics computation work by the government. As in so many scientific breakthroughs, brainstorming and camaraderie led to discoveries.

Faster and Better

In 1940, John Mauchly, a physics professor at Ursinus College, attended a conference of the American Association for the Advancement of Science, where he delivered a paper on weather statistics using his invention in digital electronic circuitry. Other scientists at the meeting, interested in Mauchly's work, conferred with him and compared notes on their own developments in electronic computing.

A graduate student in the Moore School, J. Presper Eckert, Jr., had already patented an electronic device for measuring magnetic fields that had been adopted by the U.S. Navy. He and Mauchly discussed their ideas over coffee and dessert at the now-defunct Linton's restaurant and at the university.

Together, Mauchly and Eckert created a way to find faster methods to compute ballistics. Mauchly envisioned an electronic machine that could perform 1,000 multiplications per second. (Today, computers perform more than a billion calculations per second.) Mauchly's original proposal included the ability of his device to produce ballistics tables and also included a device that was a more general-purpose digital computer and not limited to ballistics computations.

The Moore School already had a Bush differential analyzer, a sophisticated calculating device similar to but of larger capacity than one already in existence at the Ordnance Department of the U.S. Army at Aberdeen. To improve the Army Ballistic Research Laboratory's capacity for computation because of the country's involvement in World War II, the Army awarded a contract to the university. On June 5, 1942, the trustees of the university signed the contract with the U.S. Army Ordnance Department to develop this project. The proposal Mauchly and Eckert submitted to the Army as a result of the contract, titled "Project PX," proposed a fully electronic computer that could compute ballistic trajectory in under five minutes. The result was ENIAC.

BOMB SCIENTISTS GET IN THE ACT

The computer wasn't completed until 1945, so it wasn't of much use for the creation of the atom bomb, but it was used extensively for calculations in the design of the hydrogen bomb. Scientists were sent to Philadelphia to create the first set of nuclear physics calculations to be run on an all-electronic computer modeled after ENIAC.

A Giant Secret

The project was encased in secrecy. By 1944, the team of engineers working on the project could demonstrate ENIAC's workability. The inventors had to halt the project at a certain point to see if it worked, but they continued to consider a more sophisticated computer, particularly in the area of increased memory. While working on ENIAC, they tried to figure out how to store programs, but that was not to happen until later. The more sophisticated computer would increase the speed of calculations and use stored memory.

ENIAC was formally dedicated in February 1946. After the war, while the military maintained interest in ENIAC's possibilities regarding nuclear weapons development, private industry quickly saw the enormous potential for computers in the private sector. And the rest is history.

SAY CHEESE

The throw-away camera was a century and a half away when, on an October afternoon in 1839, Joseph Saxton, a mechanic who worked at the U.S. Mint, constructed a homemade camera, housed it in a cigar box, and aimed it at the nearest building. The result was the first American daguerreotype, a view of Central High School for Boys and the Pennsylvania State Arsenal, adjacent to the school's original site at the southeast corner of Centre Square and Juniper Street (now the site of the Lord and Taylor department store, formerly John Wanamaker's).

Professor Paul Beck Goddard, of the University of Pennsylvania School of Medicine, made the first successful attempt at interior photography in the mid-1840s; he photographed a human face. The public at large was thrilled with Goddard's accomplishment. But not so portrait artists, who considered it to be the beginning of the end of portraiture.

Shedding Light on the Picture

William G. Mason, an engraver who fashioned a daguerreotype of a Chestnut Street scene in 1843, is credited with taking the first perfect picture with artificial light. Photography continued to develop speedily. In 1851, Frederick and William Langenheim, photographers and inventors of photographic equipment, created the first stereoscope, a device that views two photos taken at slightly different angles so that when the two images are combined, they give an impression of depth. This device had a hooded lens, a handle, and an adjustable card holder.

FLOWERS AND PLANTS MORE THAN A GARDEN MAKE

By the mid-18th century, botanist John Bartram had made a name for himself collecting plants for patrons in England who wanted to acquire native American specimens. Bartram's original property, purchased in 1728, was a 102-acre farm on the banks of the Schuylkill. Bartram was a working farmer, but when he saw the rich and varied number of native plants in the

The home of first botanist John Bartram, situated in Historic Bartram's Garden. *Courtesy of Historic Bartram's Garden*

New World that were unknown to Europeans, he started a botanical garden, which is now the oldest botanical garden in the country.

ROYAL RECOGNITION

John Bartram's contributions to botany were considered so important, he was appointed American botanist to King George III.

One day, while plowing his fields, Bartram was moved by the sight of a beautiful daisy. That moment inspired him and his son, William, to begin a project that would last for the rest of their lives—collecting plants. Bartram used every opportunity when not farming to satisfy his botanical curiosities; he traveled the East Coast to find rare specimens, going as far north as Lake Ontario, as far south as what is now Florida, and as far west as the Ohio River.

Bartram's original garden, started in 1730, grew into one of the most important collections of American plants in the colonies. Descendants of some of these plants and trees still exist in Bartram's Garden, including *Franklinia alatamaha*, a tree now extinct in the wild.

Plants Breed Publications

In 1751, Bartram published the first American work on botany, *Observations on the Inhabitants, Climate, Soil, Divers Productions, Animals, etc., made in his travels from Pennsylvania to Onondaga, Oswego, and the Lake Ontario*. This book was the product of Bartram's 1743 travels to collect plants, which are regarded as the first scientific exploration by an American.

Among Bartram's other firsts was the publication of the first nursery catalog, entitled "Bartram's Garden Catalogue of North American Plants." It was published in 1783 by his sons, who had continued his botanical work. It included specimens that still rank among the nation's favorites, such as rhododendrons, azaleas, magnolias, and dogwoods.

A PHILADELPHIA EASTER LILY

The Easter lily was introduced to this country in 1879, when it was brought from Bermuda to Philadelphia by Mary Rogers. She propagated it for three years, until she had 100 live specimens. William K. Harris, a florist, introduced it in both Philadelphia and New York. As a result of Rogers' work, florists sometimes call Philadelphia "the city of the Easter lily."

☞ To Visit: Historic Bartram's Garden

Bartram's gardens and pre–Revolutionary War house are maintained by the John Bartram Association.

Historic Bartram's Garden
54th Street and Lindbergh Boulevard
Philadelphia, PA 19143
215-729-5281
Hours: Garden open daily. House open April-December, Wednesday-Sunday, 12-4 P.M.; January-March, Wednesday-Friday, 12-4 P.M.
Admission: Garden, free; fee charged for house and tours.
Group tours (10 or more) arranged any time.

Christopher Witt, the Mystical Herbalist

Bartram's interest in botany was preceded by some years by Dr. Christopher Witt, who joined the theosophical colonists on the Wissahickon in 1704. He started what is regarded as the first botanical garden in America. He and Bartram visited each other regularly and compared plants and theories.

WILLIAM PENN MAKES BOTANY IMPORTANT

William Penn's pronouncement of Philadelphia as a "Greene Country Towne" in 1682 was taken seriously by the University of Pennsylvania in 1768, when it established the first Department of Botany at a university in the United States.

Witt was a physician with interests in philosophy, magic, divinity, and horoscopes. He was a follower of Johannes Kelpius, leader of the mystics who settled along the Wissahickon. While Bartram was somewhat discomfited by the doctor's interest in mysticism, he respected Witt's intelligence and botanical interests, so he tolerated his fascination with astrology and magic. Bartram wrote to a friend in London of Witt's plants and the advice Witt gave him about his own garden, saying that "he hath attained the greatest knowledge in botany of any I have discoursed with."

Witt was quite a character. When he died at age 90, he was considered the last of the Rosicrucian mystics of Germantown. In addition to his work as a physician and botanist, he was also a talented mechanic, building the first clocks made in Pennsylvania, and possibly in the nation.

FIRST PUBLIC GARDEN

The Philadelphia Zoological Garden was the first public garden in America, predating the animals by almost 90 years. It began as a private garden owned by John Penn, William's grandson. In 1785, he built The Solitude, a small estate on the Schuylkill, and created an English landscape garden there. Penn's grandson was a solitary fellow, and the house he built was practically in a wilderness at the time. The original property had an extensive kitchen garden surrounding a two-story kitchen. The landscape was carefully planned to conform to the property's contours, and included many specimens of trees.

An English elm from Penn's time, which many believe started from a root shoot, remains on the property. Eventually, the property and gardens became part of Fairmount Park and the Philadelphia Zoo. Penn's house was restored in 1976 and is now a monument to colonial history and architecture, but it is not open to the public.

LET THERE BE LIGHT

When Benjamin Franklin was conducting his scientific experiments in electricity, he said, "I never was before engaged in any study that so totally engrossed my attention and my time as this has lately done . . . ." His "Philadelphia Experiments" resulted in the discovery of electricity. We think of Franklin as an inventor and a statesman, but possibly his most significant role was that of scientist.

Franklin's single-fluid theory of electricity and his proof that there are electric sparks in lightning—which resulted in the invention of the lightning rod—placed him and his home, Philadelphia, at the forefront of modern technology.

Franklin Does It Again

On June 15, 1752, Franklin demonstrated his theory that lightning and electricity are the same by drawing lightning from the clouds with a key and a kite during a lightning storm. His letter describing his experiments was read before the Royal Society of London that December. Legend has it that the experiment took place on a lot on the east side of Ridge Road, near the intersection with Buttonwood Street, and that Franklin was assisted by his son William.

HOW HOT WAS IT?

Benjamin Franklin's colleague, Ebenezer Kinnersley, invented an electrical air thermometer, which proved that electricity produces heat.

The first electrical show took place in September and October of 1884. The Electrical Exhibition and National Conference of Electricians was sponsored by the Franklin Institute. On that occasion, Thomas Edison increased the staying power of the light bulb to 400 hours, proving that his incandescent lamp was the ultimate lighting invention of its day. Soon, electric light poles dotted the streets of Philadelphia. Business saw the potential, and in 1882, the Brush Electric Light Company offered to light Chestnut Street from river to river, free of charge, as a demonstration of how well the system worked. It wasn't long after that that the city began granting franchises to private companies to provide street lighting.

THE WANAMAKER EAGLE IS ILLUMINATED

John Wanamaker installed the first electric light in a commercial store. The year was 1878.

EXPLORING THE ARCTIC

On March 4, 1753, the first North American expedition for Arctic exploration sailed from Philadelphia. The schooner *Argo*, captained by Charles Swaine, was fitted out by money raised through subscriptions from wealthy citizens of the city, who were spurred on by the unsuccessful attempts of the British to find a Northwest Passage to the Orient. A reward of £2,000 was offered to any ship that made a successful voyage.

The *Argo* got as far as Cape Farewell and the Hudson Strait, but was forced to return because of ice. The ship tried the journey again in 1754, but was once more unlucky; three of the ship's men were killed by Indians on the Labrador coast. The crew aborted its trip and returned to Philadelphia in October of that year. But the *Argo*'s attempts were not completely in vain. The expedition accurately charted the Labrador coast and discovered good fishing banks previously unknown to the colonists.

FOR THE ADVANCEMENT OF SCIENCE

The first national scientific organization was founded in this city on September 20, 1848. It was the American Association for the Advancement of Science (AAAS), and its establishment marked the beginning of a national scientific community in the United States. This group gathered together, for the first time, scientists and engineers who were working primarily on their own, with little communication between them. Eighty-seven distinguished scientists formed the organization to promote the exchange of information, cultivate science throughout the United States, and provide a more systematic direction to research. As Alexander Dallas Bache, a great-grandson of Benjamin Franklin, said in 1851, "While science is without organization, it is without power."

Even Scientists Need Direction

The group, made up of the movers and shakers of the scientific community, met in the library of the Academy of Natural Sciences. Founding members included Bache, Louis Agassiz, Joseph Henry, William Redfield, and Benjamin Silliman, Jr. Some interested laypeople also joined—Henry David Thoreau and former U.S. president Millard Fillmore were among them—and so did a few women, including Margaretta Morris of Germantown.

MORE FIRSTS

☆ Professor James Woodhouse conducted the **first experiments in burning coal as fuel** at the University of Pennsylvania and also demonstrated that oxygen was given off by living plants. He earned a medical degree from the university in 1791.

☆ Joseph Wharton of Philadelphia was the **first person to produce pure malleable nickel**, in 1876. He exhibited wrought nickel products, such as bars, rods, a cube, and a horseshoe magnet, and magnetic needles of forged nickel at the Centennial Exhibition.

☆ **Pneumatic mailing tubes**, used in department stores before the era of credit cards and still used by some banks today, were first introduced in this country in Philadelphia in 1892.

☆ University of Pennsylvania provost Edgar Fahs Smith **first used tungsten in incandescent light bulbs** at the university.

☆ The American Philosophical Society created a forum for scientific papers and inventions, and on April 20, 1940, the society was the **first to see a demonstration of an electron microscope.** The 10-foot-high instrument could magnify a specimen up to 100,000 times its size.

SUGGESTED READINGS

Bowen, Catherine Drinker. *Miracle at Philadelphia*. Boston: Little, Brown, 1966.

Brookhouser, Frank. *Our Philadelphia*. New York: Doubleday, 1957.

Cotter, John I., Daniel G. Roberts, and Michael Parrington. *The Buried Past: An Archaeological History of Philadelphia*. Philadelphia: University of Pennsylvania Press, 1992.

Federal Writers' Project. *WPA Guide to Philadelphia, 1988 edition*. Philadelphia: University of Pennsylvania Press, 1988.

Repplier, Agnes. *Philadelphia, the Place and the People*. New York: Macmillan, 1898.

Smith, Philip, and Chadwick Foster. *Philadelphia on the River*. Philadelphia: Philadelphia Maritime Museum, 1986.

Snyder, Martin P. *City of Independence*. New York: Praeger Publishers, 1975.

Weigley, Russel F., ed. *Philadelphia: A 300-Year History*. New York: W. W. Norton, 1982.

Wolf, Edwin 2nd. *Philadelphia: Portrait of an American City*. Philadelphia: Camino Books, 1990.